Title IX Indian Education Project
Sioux City Community Schools
1221 Pierce
Sioux City, Iowa 51105-1497

AMERICAN
INDIAN LIVES

ARTISTS
AND
CRAFTSPEOPLE

◆ ◆ ◆

Arlene Hirschfelder

Facts On File®

AN INFOBASE HOLDINGS COMPANY

To Dennis, Adam, and Brooke for their love and support

◆ ◆ ◆

On the cover: (left) Bill Reid; (right) Nampeyo

Artists and Craftspeople

Copyright © 1994 by Arlene Hirschfelder

Facts On File, Inc.
460 Park Avenue South
New York NY 10016

Library of Congress Cataloging-in-Publication Data

Hirschfelder, Arlene B.
    Artists and craftspeople / Arlene Hirschfelder.
        p. cm. — (American Indian lives)
    Includes bibliographical references and index.
    ISBN 0-8160-2960-1
    1. Indian artists—United States—Biography—Juvenile literature.
    2. Indian artists—Canada—Biography—Juvenile literature.
    [1. Artists. 2. Indians of North America—Biography.] I. Title.
    II. Series: American Indian lives (New York, N.Y.)
    E98.A7H57   1994
    709′ .2′273—dc20
    [B]   93–46049

Text design by Ellen Levine
Cover design by Nora Wertz
Printed in the United States of America

MP FOF 10 9 8 7 6 5 4 3 2 1

This book is printed on acid-free paper.

CONTENTS

◆ ◆ ◆

ACKNOWLEDGMENTS

◆ ◆ ◆

To Leslie Frank McKeon for her many talents, especially her enthusiasm, knowledge, and assistance in researching and writing Nampeyo and Maria Martinez.

*A portion of the author's royalties will be donated to Atlatl,
a non-profit Native American arts service organization.*

◆ ◆ ◆

INTRODUCTION

◆ ◆ ◆

Native Americans have always beautified their everyday lives. Before contact with Euroamericans, unknown and unnamed Native men and women skillfully shaped and richly decorated their belongings. Made with a tremendous range of natural materials and a wealth of ingenuity, clothing, tools, food bowls, cups, ladles, jars, containers, and dozens of other everyday and ceremonial objects became true artistic triumphs. The surface decorations often expressed a reverence for and special relationship with the natural world. Since Native peoples depended on animals, fish, and plants, their art honored these living things for their role in the cycle of life.

Native art also was grounded in ancient rituals and oral traditions from hundreds of different Native American groups living throughout North America. Experienced elders taught younger generations the skills necessary to make containers from plants or clay, carve wooden masks, and paint animal hides. Equally important, Native elders shared stories and attitudes that, while invisible in the design of a pot or basket, nevertheless maintained the heart of Native cultures. Nature-oriented elders made sure that members of the next generation understood their relationship to plants, animals, water, and land that sustains life. Elders made sure the next generation knew the ritual acts to perform before creating a basket, mask, or article of clothing. Before carving a sacred wooden mask from a tree struck by lightning, Zunis prepared it in special ways, "addressed" it, and "fed" the tree with ceremonial tobacco. Zunis believed the rituals to be just as important as the technical skills required to carve the mask. Today, many Native

American artists continue their ancient traditions. A potter may offer prayers before firing a pot, a basket maker may pray while collecting grasses.

Just as traditional Native life did not need to establish formal art schools neither did it establish museums or art galleries. Native peoples did not single out anyone as gifted because he or she created beautiful designs on clothing or household objects. Making things look beautiful was such a natural part of life that most Indian languages did not have words for "art" or "artist."

Before Europeans arrived, Native groups borrowed ideas, materials, designs, and objects from other Native groups whose lifestyles, languages, and art traditions differed from their own. Athabascan-speaking Navajo women, renowned today for their woven blankets and rugs, learned weaving techniques and designs from Pueblo weavers in the aftermath of the Pueblo Revolt against the Spanish in 1680. Contact with European goods produced changes in Native cultures already accustomed to change. Native Americans substituted the wool yarn from sheep used by Euroamericans for the traditional goat wool along the northwest coast; beads for porcupine quills in the Plains; wool cloth for animal skins and furs; and silver ornaments for bone, antler, and shell whenever and wherever they could trade for these items.

After contact with Euroamericans, Native art changed. Some of it is vastly different from objects created by Native peoples more than a hundred years ago. Some of it still resembles the beautiful objects made centuries before. Some of it combines the old with the new. Native artists are now painting on canvas, beading (Europeans brought glass beads to the Americas) sneakers and baseball caps, quilting (wives of missionaries and settlers pieced together scraps of cloth) blankets, printmaking, making three-dimensional jewelry, and welding steel into sculpture.

Native art, at one time a tribal expression reflecting a group's traditions, lore, and symbols, has now become an individually oriented expression that is highly collectible. The work of well-known artists is sought by collectors, a phenomenon unknown in pre-European contact times when the names of people creating baskets, pottery, and carved masks were not recorded. Because collectors purchasing art measure the importance of paintings, pottery, or baskets by the particular artist who creates them, Indians have adapted the tradition of signing their works to please the consumers, increase the value of objects, and help them sell. World-famous potter Maria Martinez, who was persuaded by consumers to sign her works, signed not only her own pots but sometimes those made by other women from San Ildefonso Pueblo. Eager to help her relatives make a living from their pottery, Martinez knew her signature elevated prices. This practice started as early as the late 1870s. A group of Cheyenne, Arapaho, Kiowa, and Comanche men imprisoned at Fort Marion in Saint Augustine, Florida, began selling to tourists their drawings of daily tribal life, hunting, and warfare scenes. Most of the artist-prisoners put some kind of signature or mark on their works.

Artists and Craftspeople introduces readers to pictographic art and its legacy and 17 gifted Native American artists of the 20th century each of whom has made significant contributions either to the field of basket weaving, carving, doll making, jewelry, pottery, painting, or sculpture. An effort was made to include men and women from different tribes and from different regions of the United States and Canada. Whatever the art form, the artists in this volume have either stayed close to their tribal heritages or departed from them while still drawing on them for ideas and inspiration. Because of its size, this book has limits. It simply was not possible to be comprehensive and include every basket weaver, carver, painter, and so on. Space limitations also meant eliminating a number of important art forms. Additional volumes are needed to explore textile artists (including Navajo woven rugs and blankets, Seminole patchwork, Great Lake Native ribbon appliqué, northern Plains Indian morning star quilts, Northwest Coast button blankets), flute makers, drum makers, photographers, printmakers, Inuit artists who make fur clothing, clothing artists who make powwow regalia, and artists who have revived the art of making wampum (shell made into tube-shaped beads that are fashioned into belts and necklaces), porcupine quillwork, and parfleche (rawhide containers).

These essays do not contain long passages with technical explanations about the ways to hand build a pot, plait a basket, carve limestone, or weld steel. Technical manuals provide those answers. Nor do these essays offer the views of art critics who pick apart an artist's carving, painting, or piece of jewelry. Books written by experts in Native art forms provide those kinds of analysis. What the essays do focus on are details and events in the artists' lives that shaped their artistic expressions. Based on written sources and, in some cases, interviews, each essay follows the artist from birth through childhood, schooling, and adulthood, zeroing in on when, how, and why the artists learned their particular art form. The essays consider the influential roles of parents, grandparents, and other relatives. Other influences shaped the artists so archaeologists, non-Indian teachers, U.S. government policies, World War II, boarding schools, art patrons, collectors, galleries, museums, abstract expressionism, trading posts, junkyards, and the basic need to make a living figure in the stories as well. Finally, each essay mentions the names of museums and art galleries in the United States and Canada where readers may go see the paintings, baskets, sculpture, and other works discussed in the volume.

DAT SO LA LEE

◆ ◆ ◆

Washo Basket Maker
(c. 1835 or 1850 – 1925)

*. . . Dat So La Lee created a more reserved style of profound
visual poetry.*
—Erwin L. Wade,
in *The Arts of the North American Indian* (1986)

Dabuda was a Washo Indian, known at first by her legal name,
Louisa Keyser, the surname of her second husband, and after 1900
by her nickname Dat So La Lee, which was believed to mean "big
hips" in Washo. Since she eventually weighed some 300 pounds,
this name would have described her.

Born sometime between 1835 and 1850, according to the best
guesses of scholars who have studied her life, Dabuda lived in a
village near the mining town of Sheridan, Nevada. Originally, the
Washo settled in small valleys along the eastern side of the Sierra
Nevada range and around Lake Tahoe on the border of Nevada
and California. Scholars who have studied Dabuda's life have not
turned up anything about her parents. She grew up in a traditional
way, learning from older women how to gather food, cook it, and
make baskets.

Washo people used baskets from morning to night, from "the
cradle to the grave." Older Washo women showed Dabuda how
to gather the best plant materials to make the containers as well as
how to turn the plant fibers into weaving threads. Like other

Washo women, Dabuda became a skilled botanist. She knew when and where to gather the materials she needed to make weaving threads. She needed these skills. Before contact with Euroamericans and their manufactured utensils, Washo women bathed their babies on basket-like trays and put them to sleep on pillows and cradles made from baskets. They made children's toys from baskets and made conical ("burden") baskets that they strapped on their backs to carry the acorns and seeds they gathered. They made large baskets to store the harvested seeds and nuts and household objects, made scoop-shaped baskets for winnowing (separating grain). They also made conical baskets to use in Washo ceremonies. They cooked mush in baskets by heating rocks in a fire, picking them up with wooden tongs, and dropping them into cooking baskets filled with water and meal. People ate from baskets and drank from them. Women coated baskets with pitch so they could hold water. Families lived in homes made from twigs and braided basketry. They caught fish with basket nets and weirs and animals with basket snares and traps. When Washo men died, their baskets were buried with them. When Washo women died, large burden baskets were placed upside down on their graves. Women decorated the upper parts of their baskets with designs of triangles, diamonds, lines, and zigzags in black, a color derived from mud-dyed roots of bracken fern, and red, from redbud branches. These they imported from the Miwok people to the west who used redbud in their basketry.

During the second half of the 19th century, when Dabuda was growing up, the Washo people saw thousands of Euroamerican settlers come and rapidly change their lives. The settlers took over Washo lands in the valleys, cut their trees for houses, grazed cattle on the grasses, put up fences, laid down roads and railroads, cut off game trails, killed off fish by polluting streams with waste from mining, and infected them with Euroamerican diseases. Soon the Washo, deprived of their traditional way of living, moved near white settlements to work for white families. By the turn of the century Washo lifestyle had drastically changed as a result of working in towns and on ranches. Women did laundry and men worked outside doing chores and farm labor. Since Washo people could now use Euroamerican-manufactured household pots and pans, they did not need to make baskets to store food, cart acorns, or carry water. Slowly, the tradition of making baskets declined.

Around 1871, Dabuda went to the mining town of Monitor, in Alpine County, California, and worked for a while for Harris Cohn, his wife, and family. More than 20 years later, the Cohns' son, Abe, was to play a major role in Dabuda's life. After working in Monitor, Dabuda lived on the Keyser and Elrod Ranch in Carson Valley, Nevada, where she washed clothes and cooked for miners and their wives with tin pans and iron pots. Sometime during this period, she married, but her husband died. In 1888, she married for a second time. Her new husband was a fellow ranch worker, Charles Keyser, a mixed blood who was 24 years younger than she. When she married Charles, Dabuda became known by her English name, Louisa Keyser, a name that came from Charles who had adopted the name Keyser from the family that owned the ranch where they worked.

In 1895, Louisa Keyser walked into Carson City, Nevada, with four willow-covered whiskey flasks and showed them to Abe Cohn, her former employer's son. That day changed her life forever and set her on a course that made her one of the most famous basket weavers in the world. Abe and Amy Cohn, who owned the Emporium Company, a men's clothing store in Carson City, bought baskets made by Washo women. It was actually Amy who loved Indian things and who turned the clothing store into a curio shop. By the late 1890s, a corner of the store was piled high with Indian artifacts, including baskets made by Washo women and Pomo women from California. The Cohns bought the baskets that women no longer used or needed in their houses. Amy and Abe had amassed quite a collection of Washo baskets, buying anything they could get their hands on. Between 1896 and 1904, they collected 300 baskets a year. For the next 30 years, they collected them at a rate of 100 a year. When the supply ran low, they hired weavers to make more.

When Louisa Keyser walked into their store carrying her willow-covered flasks, the Cohns hired her to do their laundry, but they also encouraged her to weave baskets in her spare time so they could sell them in their store. As time passed, they asked her to weave more and wash less until they offered her full patronage—the opportunity to become a full-time artist. The Cohns supported Louisa and Charles for the next 25 years, building them a home next door to theirs, paying for their food, fuel, clothing, and medical expenses. In return for the Cohns' total financial support, they owned every basket Louisa made.

The baskets Louisa made for the Cohns had three colors derived from natural fibers. In the fall, she gathered long, straight branches of willow and, using her fingernails and teeth, stripped them of their bark. Willow's inner fiber, below the bark and above the pith, provided tan or white weaving threads. She also used willow branches as the foundation sticks of her baskets. In the spring, she went to the western slope of the Sierras and dug up well-developed roots of the bracken fern. She buried the dark brown roots in mud for two weeks to turn them black, shredding the inner stock of the roots to make black threads. In the summer, she carefully gathered red bark from redbud when it was red and lustrous and shredded it to make reddish threads. Louisa rolled each variety of strand into balls, tied them, and allowed them to cure (dry) and season for her next year's work. She made her baskets from the threads that were prepared the year before. Louisa had slender hands and delicate fingers that were always cut and sore from shredding plant fibers. She endured eye strain and backaches while making her masterpieces.

Soon after the Cohns started supporting her work, Louisa introduced, in 1896, a new basket shape that looked traditional but wasn't and that transformed Washo basket weaving into a renowned art style. This newly created basket was made solely to be sold, a far cry from Washo tradition where every basket that was manufactured was meant to be used for a specific purpose. Abe Cohn called this basket *degikup* (day-gee-coop), which resembles a Washo sound. The word refers to the shape of the basket, which is spherical, with a small mouth. Louisa made her style of degikup throughout her career and resisted any other innovations. Over time, she increased the size of her degikup. As

Portrait of renowned Washo basket weaver Dat So La Lee, also known as Louisa Keyser, taken by Amy Cohn in 1897. (Photograph courtesy of National Museum of the American Indian, Smithsonian Institution)

they grew in size, so, too, did the time it took to complete one. Months passed, even a year, before she finished an intricately designed, finely woven degikup.

Louisa made most of her degikup baskets with three willow sticks as the foundation over which she coiled her threads. She refined the shape of traditional Washo baskets and expanded the design to cover most of the surface. She paid attention to the inside of her baskets. They were as attractive as the outside. For almost 20 years, she decorated almost every work with a scatter pattern, small multiple geometric forms repeated all over the surface. Some scholars believe that the scatter patterns used by Pomo basket weavers inspired her. Since Cohn's Emporium sold Pomo baskets, Louisa had ample opportunity to study them.

Although Louisa spent most of her time making degikup, she produced other kinds of baskets as well. She wove traditional sorting and burden baskets, miniatures, cradles, covered bottles and flasks, belts, fish carriers, and baskets for sacred objects. Even with her miniatures, she covered the surface with her scattered designs.

From the beginning, the Cohns kept records of Louisa's baskets, marking each of the 121 baskets in a registry with her initials, "L.K." (for Louisa Keyser) and a number. When a customer bought a basket, the Cohns' bill of sale included Louisa's hand print, a description of the basket, the number of stitches to the inch, the name of the design, and the time it took her to construct the vessel. The Cohns named the baskets with long descriptive subtitles like "Myriads of stars shine over the graves of our ancestors" or "Our men camped beside the roads and rivers, then assembled around the campfires praising and extolling the shrewdness and skill of their hunters in obtaining game of earth and air."

Amy Cohn, who exhibited Louisa's baskets in the summer of 1900 in Nevada and California, developed a promotional pamphlet that doubled as a certificate. Issued with the purchase of a basket, it cited Louisa Keyser's name (until she became known after 1900 as Dat So La Lee); date of completion; the technique and materials used to make the basket; and its design name, size, and weight.

In 1918, Amy started a separate ledger for Dat So La Lee's baskets. For the baskets Dat So La Lee wove before 1899, Amy simply manufactured information. In fact, Amy manufactured lots of information about Dat So La Lee herself. First off, of all the Washo women making baskets for Cohn's Emporium, Dat So La

Lee was the only weaver known by a Washo name. The Cohns wanted her to look like a traditional Washo woman, even though her relationship to the Cohns was not at all traditional. Amy Cohn called her a traditional weaver, not admitting that Dat So La Lee wove degikup baskets for sale, which was not a traditional practice at all. Amy claimed that Dat So La Lee had preserved the knowledge of degikup weaving from precontact times, which was not true. She claimed degikup were traditional mortuary baskets and made up a fictitious burial ceremony to make the story more believable.

In fact, Amy Cohn went even further. She claimed Dat So La Lee alone inherited the right as a Washo "princess" to weave degikup and claimed she wove the history and traditional stories of her people into the basketry patterns. For example, in one certificate, Amy provided the following information about the large basket called "Beacon Lights," woven between July 1904 and September 1905, which had flame motifs in red and black in a scatter pattern: "large signal fires or beacon lights were built upon the high hills to call absent members of the Washo tribe together for consultation as danger threatened." On March 31, 1914, a Pennsylvania man bought "Beacon Lights" for $1,400. The Cohns reported to the newspapers that he paid close to $2,000. The publicity helped the Cohns sell a degikup for $600 in 1917.

Whenever Amy Cohn lectured about Dat So La Lee's baskets, she wore a fringed buckskin dress, recited Indian legends, and gave her made-up interpretations of Dat So La Lee's designs. Amy also ran a branch store of the Emporium on Lake Tahoe called the Bicose—the Washo word for baby carrier. From June to September, Dat So La Lee and her husband lived there in another home Abe provided for them. She was expected to demonstrate her basket weaving in public to attract customers. Since Lake Tahoe attracted upper-class people who could afford high-priced baskets, the Cohns sold baskets to tourists through their summer shop.

Abe also made up stories about Dat So La Lee that were published in newspapers edited by his friends. He focused on his relationship to her, stressing how he helped provide support for this "helpless" woman. He said Dat So La Lee was childish, lacking common sense, and unable to control her emotions. Abe and Amy did more than tell their made-up tales to customers and local newspapers. In November of 1919, they took Dat So La Lee by train to the Industrial Arts Exposition in St. Louis. There she was put on display and had to demonstrate her basket weaving. Dat So La Lee was the subject of many feature articles in magazines and newspapers, which enabled Abe Cohn to sell more of her baskets.

Amy Cohn died in the winter of 1919 shortly after returning from the St. Louis Exposition. Cohn's second wife was less interested in baskets, so Abe promoted them himself. In 1922, he had a film made of Dat So La Lee gathering and preparing her materials and demonstrating her techniques.

In 1925, shortly before Dat So La Lee died, Edward Curtis, a renowned photographer, visited Cohn's Emporium. He photographed the basket weaver with her works for his monumental study *The North American Indians*. Soon after, Dat So La Lee, suffering from dropsy, refused to go to the Stewart Indian Hospital. She was taken by a taxi to a shelter near Lone Mountain where a medicine man attended her. She eventually died December 6, 1925 and was buried in the Stewart Indian School Cemetery along with her last degikup and other treasured items. Her husband lived another three years.

By the time Dat So La Lee died, her baskets were selling for as much as $5,000 apiece, an enormous sum of money. Today, her baskets can be found in a number of American museums. The Nevada State Museum in Carson City and the Nevada Historical Society in Reno both have major collections.

NAMPEYO

◆ ◆ ◆

Hopi Potter
(c. 1859–1942)

The Old Lady [Nampeyo] told us that we should learn to make
pottery because it would be something to provide us a living.
She knew this was true for her children and grandchildren and
also for all Hopi potters. She had the vision to know this, and
it has proven to be true. She was concerned with all the Hopi,
not just her own family.
     —Nampeyo's grandchild to John F. Collins,
        in *Nampeyo, Hopi Potter*

Nampeyo was born in the village of Hano in Hopi country
sometime around 1859. Just as Anglo-Americans usually take their
father's family name when they are born, Hopi children traditionally belong to their mother's clan, so Nampeyo was a member of
the Corn Clan, but, according to Hopi custom, was named by her
father's mother. Since her father was a member of the Snake Clan,
her grandmother named the baby girl Tcu-mana, which means
Snake Girl in the Hopi language. But the people of Hano, who
speak the Tewa language, called the little girl Nampeyo, which
means the same thing in their language.

The Hopi live on the high plateau of northern Arizona. In this
harsh and remote environment, the Hopi mesas remained relatively free of Spanish and, later, Mexican domination. Around
1700, the Tewa people, fleeing hunger and Spanish domination,

left the Rio Grande region of New Mexico and settled in Hano village on First Mesa. Though their lives and culture became permanently intertwined with the Hopi, they maintained their own language and history and lore. Today Hano is one of the few villages where people still speak the Tewa language. When the New Mexico territory (which included Arizona) was acquired by the United States in 1848 after the war with Mexico, the Hopi and Hopi-Tewa people held onto their traditional ways. Even today they maintain the lifestyle, beliefs, and traditions of their ancestors to a remarkable degree. It was into this Indian world that Nampeyo was born more than 50 years before Arizona became one of the United States. Nampeyo never studied at an Anglo school. She never learned to read, write, or speak English and never learned Anglo ways. She never had an English name. All her life Nampeyo remained, first and foremost, a Hopi woman who happened to be a potter, rather than a potter who happened to be Hopi.

The Hopi mesas, where the people live in apartment-like pueblos or villages, stick up like three spines on the high plateau. Like a mountain ridge with no trees, they are exposed to the elements, the hot summer sun, fierce storms and the bitter winter wind and snow. High in the big open sky, with the vast desert stretched out to the horizon in all directions, much of Hopi life was devoted to survival and living in harmony with the harsh and beautiful environment. This required cooperation and the effort of the whole community. Individualism and competition, so greatly admired in the Anglo-American world, were discouraged.

As a child, Nampeyo learned the ways and traditions of her people, as did all Hopi children. She learned the skills she would need to be a successful Hopi woman, to cook the flat, blue "piki" corn bread, to gather wild foods, to help construct the homes, and do the mud plastering required to maintain them. And she learned pottery making, also women's work, long practiced by both her Hopi and Tewa ancestors.

Nampeyo's Hopi grandmother was a recognized potter and Nampeyo watched and learned from working with her. She learned by imitation of and with encouragement from her grandmother because that was the traditional Hopi method of teaching. She learned how to make pots "from scratch," because that, too, was the Hopi way. Nampeyo gathered clay from the earth below the mesa. She sifted out the sticks and stones, ground the clay on a metate (a stone used for grinding), mixed it with sand or crushed pot shards so that it could be molded, and added the right amount of water. She learned by practice and by feel the right amount of each ingredient.

Nampeyo learned to make pottery in the traditional way of her ancestors. The Hopi and other Indians built pottery by hand. A small pot could be pinched in the potter's hands. A larger pot was made by coiling. First a small ball of clay was flattened into a pancake and placed on the ground on a "puki"—any rounded bowl shape, perhaps a broken pot or a tin saucer. Then Nampeyo learned to make long, snake-like coils. Each coil would be attached, one after the other, to the base on the puki and pinched around the whole circle to hold the different pieces together. If the clay got too dry, it would crack and crumble, so a potter always kept a bowl of water at her side. Too much water and the walls would collapse. After the pot was shaped, Nampeyo would scrape and then polish, or burnish, it to a shiny finish with a smooth stone.

As she worked, Nampeyo would hold up her bowl to study the shape. Pots should be perfectly symmetrical, smooth and graceful, with walls of even thickness. A pot should not have a thin, delicate rim and be surprisingly bottom heavy when lifted.

In 1875 the U.S. government sent surveyors and photographers to the New Mexico territory. On First Mesa William Henry Jackson photographed a girl who captured for him the image of the people who lived in this dramatic country. The picture was widely reproduced throughout the United States. It showed a young girl, small, about 15 years old, wearing her hair in large whorls, one over each ear, called "squash blossom" or "butterfly," which indicated that she was ready for marriage. The picture was of Nampeyo. So long before anyone knew who she was, they knew what she looked like.

Shortly after she was photographed, Nampeyo married Kwivoya, but the marriage never worked. Around 1881 she married Lesou with whom she lived for some 50 years until he died.

They had five or more children and he probably helped greatly with the development of the pottery style that Nampeyo made famous. But we know little about him.

During this time, contact between the Hopi and outside American culture was increasing rapidly. Traders moved into Indian country and set up trading posts to buy and sell with the Indians. One was established at Keams Canyon, 12 miles north of First Mesa, and Nampeyo probably began selling her pottery there.

Most likely Nampeyo found and studied potsherds, pieces of old pottery, from old pueblo settlements—Awatovi, Jeddito, and Sikyatki—abandoned some two and three centuries earlier. When she went down the mesa to get clay or water she would pass nearby, and it was quite possible that she found shards. Possibly these fragments of designs and pots began influencing Nampeyo from her youth. Some scholars think that pots she made in the 1870s and 1880s were quite similar to ones she made later. But we don't really know when particular pots were made since Nampeyo never signed or dated her work.

We do know that at the time Nampeyo was born the quality of Hopi pottery had declined severely and was worse than it had been in centuries. Made mainly for cooking, storage, and other practical functions, it was often chunky, poorly made, undecorated or crudely decorated. With the arrival of cheap Anglo-American tins and bowls, the craft might well have passed into oblivion.

As United States expansion continued, anthropologists came to study the Indians, archaeologists came to dig up their past, and explorers, settlers, and adventurers of all kinds came to seek their fortunes. The expansion of the Santa Fe Railroad opened the country to anyone who wanted to come.

In 1895, Jesse Fewkes, a young Harvard graduate, arrived to begin excavating the old Hopi village of Sikyatki, about a mile from Hano. Several Hopi men got jobs at the dig. Lesou was one of them. Large quantities of multi-colored finely painted pots and shards were dug up, some from settlements even older than Sikyatki. Lesou took some home to Nampeyo, and she was so excited that she began coming to the dig to draw and expand the

Nampeyo shown decorating pottery in 1900. (Photograph courtesy of National Anthropological Archives, Smithsonian Institution)

designs on paper. She once told Ruth Bunzel, an anthropologist, how she used to go to Sikyatki and copy the designs. "That is how I learned to paint." When Walter Hough of the Smithsonian Institute in Washington, D.C., visited Fewkes in 1896, he met Nampeyo and saw her work. He was so impressed with her artistic skills that he bought several pieces for the U.S. national museum.

Not only was Nampeyo influenced by the Sikyatki designs but she also changed the shape of her vessels to better display her new designs. She used many different forms, but the most famous and most copied form she used was a low, wide spreading jar that rounded in at the shoulder to a flat top with a round open mouth in the center. Nampeyo would paint around the top of the jar with the designs spilling gently over the shoulder. Her designs were free, loose, and uncluttered. She once told Ruth Bunzel, "the best arrangement for the water jar is four designs around the top—two and two. The designs opposite should be alike."

Nampeyo's pots derive much of their character from their earth colors, colors strongly associated with the Southwest. The background would range from a pale, creamy color to a darker buff and the designs would be painted in a red-rust and a dark umber or brown-black color. The colors come from the minerals of the earth, and Nampeyo painted them on with a homemade brush that came from the yucca plant. Firing pottery, like making pottery, was done out of doors, directly on the ground. On a good morning, when the air was dry and still, Nampeyo carefully stacked the pots, surrounded them by local wood and animal dung as fuel, and set the mound aflame.

Nampeyo's commercial success inspired other Hano potters to follow her example. Unlike many Anglo-American artists, Nampeyo freely shared her ideas and techniques. That was the Hopi way, and soon all the Hano potters were making and selling Sikyatki revival pottery. Many Hopi people in the other villages, accustomed to trading for the traditional Hano-type pottery, criticized the change as ugly. But the women of Hano were happy selling their pots to the traders and other Euroamericans for money. Within a few years, the old Sikyatki revival pottery was the only pottery being made on First Mesa.

Nampeyo made three trips off the Hopi reserve. With the expansion of the Santa Fe Railroad, the Fred Harvey Company built a luxury hotel at the Grand Canyon. To keep the tourists entertained and spending money, the company also built "Hopi House," a large three-story building constructed by Hopi workers, in the style of a Hopi pueblo. In some rooms there were displays and sale of all kinds of Indian crafts. In other rooms there were rotating groups of Hopi Indians, also on display. Nampeyo and her extended family—her husband, her grown and small children, a son-in-law and grandchild—composed the first group. Advertising copy of the Harvey Company described these "quaintly garbed Indians" who demonstrated their "traditional pottery making and performed entertaining songs and dances in their traditional ceremonial style."

While she graciously demonstrated her work, posed for pictures and produced enormous quantities of pottery, Nampeyo had no desire to change her life. Homesick at the end of the three-month arrangement, Nampeyo's family wanted to return home. The Harvey Company did not want them to leave because Nampeyo's pottery was selling well, but they did anyway, in time for spring planting. Nampeyo and her family returned to Hopi House in 1907, but again they left in time to be home for planting corn.

In 1910 Nampeyo and her extended family made a trip to Chicago for a land exposition to encourage settlers and tourists to come to the Southwest. The family was required to dress in native costume, and two girls had to wear their hair in squash blossom whorls. Again, the family showed their wares, demonstrated their craft, and danced and performed.

When the United States entered World War I, tourism dropped and interest in the Southwest waned. By the end of the war, Nampeyo was getting old and going blind. She could no longer paint, but she continued to mold pottery and Lesou and their daughters did the painting. Because these were different individuals with different ways of working and seeing things, the style of painting changed. Nampeyo's loose, sweeping style was replaced by more geometric and busier designs.

When Nampeyo died in 1942, she had gained recognition in the Euroamerican world as an artist. Though she never signed her work and never sold her pots for more than a few dollars each, her descendants and other Indians are able to work and live as artists to some extent because she paved the way.

PLAINS INDIAN PICTOGRAPHIC ART AND THE KIOWA FIVE

◆ ◆ ◆

*Of all the ledger drawings, perhaps the most significant
because of their direct impact on the later development of
Native American painting, were the ones created in that most
unlikely place for an art movement, the prison of Fort Marion,
Florida—the Castillo de San Marcos of St. Augustine.*
—Arthur Silberman,
in 100 Years of Native American Painting (1978)

Miserably damp stone rooms in an old massive rock fortress
hardly seem the place for an art colony of American Indians to
have developed, yet from 1875 to 1878, that is exactly what happened. Completed in 1695, the fortress that guarded the entrance
to Saint Augustine harbor, Florida, eventually held Indians as
military prisoners at different times. During one of those periods,
homesick Indian prisoners poured their feelings out in hundreds
of drawings we now call "ledger art."

During the winter of 1873–74, in Indian Territory (present-day
Oklahoma), the Kiowa, Cheyenne, Arapaho, and Comanche peoples were starving. Game was scarce on the newly created reservation to which they were confined. When the government food
rations arrived, the beef was usually spoiled and other foods
were also inedible. And there never was enough to feed everyone. By the spring of 1874, government supplies had not arrived
at all. Lt. Colonel Thomas of the 6th Cavalry wrote: "This failure

to feed the Indians by the Indian Department . . . is in my opinion a cause of Indians leaving their reservation and going on the warpath." That's what the tribesmen did. In the winter of 1874–75, they fled the reservation to go hunt for food on ancestral lands now claimed by whites. Violence spread across the Plains. The army fought the Indians in a punishing war from July to December 1874. Soldiers burned their camps, destroyed tipis and food supplies. Freezing and starving, the Indian groups surrendered. Accused of various atrocities against Euroamericans, 72 "lawbreakers" were sentenced to three years of prison and exiled from their homelands in the western plains of the United States.

In the spring of 1875, Brevet Captain Richard H. Pratt of the United States Army escorted these 72 prisoners of war to jail in the remote Spanish fort then called Fort Marion. Held in leg irons on a long overland train ride, the warrior criminals were met by gaping crowds when the train pulled into St. Louis, Indianapolis, Nashville, Atlanta, and Jacksonville. In Jacksonville, the prisoners were moved from the railroad cars to a steamboat, which took them up the St. John's River to Tocoi. There they boarded the St. John's Railway for the last leg of their journey to the fort where they were imprisoned for the next three years. On May 21, 1875, the warriors finally arrived at Fort Marion (restored to its original name, Castillo de San Marcos, by Congress in 1942).

Not long after their arrival at Saint Augustine (at that time a resort town), Pratt removed the chains of the Indian prisoners and set about changing them into white men. That meant teaching Indians how to read English, count, think, and look like white men. He cut their hair and made them dress in army uniforms. He found them odd jobs such as shining sea beans, pale grey seeds with hard shells, that were fashioned into jewelry and sold as souvenirs to tourists. Pratt liked the Indian prisoners to keep busy so he gave them drawing books and colored pencils, crayons, and ink. He encouraged them to draw pictures to sell to Euroamericans.

At least 28 of the men, principally Kiowa and Cheyenne, spent their free time filling up army commissary books, traders' ledgers, and muslin with traditional pictographic images. These men came from tribal communities where men bragged about their heroic exploits by painting pictures on tipis, animal-hide robes, and shields for all to "read." The prisoners easily shifted the images from hide to paper while pencils and inks replaced bone brushes and earth pigments. The Fort Marion artists drew as they pleased and what pleased them most was to draw scenes they remembered of camp and reservation life on the open plains, tribal ceremonies, hunts, and battles. But they also drew scenes with western style architecture, trains, sea vessels, classrooms with teachers drilling the ABCs, beaches, and sailboats. While they eagerly experimented with space, diagonal foreshortening, and other artistic conventions, they persisted in their tribal traditions by using picture drawings (pictography) to record deeds, personal visions, historic events, and to recount their new adventures in an alien environment. Now called "ledger art," this style of art has influenced nearly all American Indians painting in the 20th century.

Wohaw, a Kiowa man born about 1855 in the southern Plains, was one of the Fort Marion artists who eagerly took to recreating his tribal past life and present reality in pictographic style. Altogether he filled two sketchbooks with 48 drawings, which have been housed at the Missouri Historical Society since 1882, plus three individual drawings now housed at the Smithsonian Institution in Washington, D.C. He began one notebook with classic scenes of warfare on the southern Plains but turned to painting scenes that had no counterpart in the older tradition of hide painting. These scenes faithfully recorded the events of his captivity. He drew Fort Sill, in Oklahoma, where the 20-year-old Wohaw and 71 other prisoners were first rounded up before being shipped to Fort Marion, scenes of train travel between Oklahoma and Florida, the various sea vessels he saw—from sidewheel boats complete with passengers to double-masted ships—and finally the massive Spanish fortress that held him captive as well as the lighthouse near Fort Marion.

Wohaw expanded the tradition of Plains hide painting by drawing scenes of courtship, ceremonies, and tribal life—a far cry from the battle scenes proud warriors usually painted on shields and tipis. He depicted three women standing alongside a dead buffalo. The women, whose role it was to butcher the dead buffalo, hold

About 1877, while a prisoner at Fort Marion in Florida, Wohaw, a young Kiowa, used traditional Plains hide painting style to convey his personal thoughts about his identity. (Photograph courtesy of Missouri Historical Society)

sharpened knives that will skin the animal. He drew a Kiowa man and woman wrapped in one blanket, a public act proclaiming their devotion to one other, and pictured a scene of the sacred Kiowa Sun Dance lodge built every June with leafy cottonwood branches covering the exterior.

Although Wohaw drew pictures in the notebooks destined for outsiders, he did not simply draw pictures that appealed to tourists. He made drawings that exposed his private thoughts and confused feelings about who he was after months of wearing army clothing, speaking, reading and writing English, and studying the Bible. Wohaw expressed his dilemma in what is now considered his most famous drawing showing him placed in the center of the page, caught between two worlds. On his right (the left side of the picture), Wohaw pictured the Plains Indian lifestyle symbolized by the buffalo, the Plains Indian staff of life, tipi, and homeland. On his left side (the right side of the picture), Wohaw, whose name translated into White Man's Spotted Cow, drew the Euroamerican lifestyle with a domestic cow, house, and cultivated field. The young man in the picture offers a pipe to both worlds, yet he faces the cow and plants his left foot on the cultivated field. Wohaw drew himself with traditional long hair and animal hide clothing and printed his own name above in English. Wohaw's drawing, with his distinctive style and signature, transformed traditional Plains art into personal expression that paved the way for Plains artists to express their individuality in the early 20th century.

In April of 1878, the prisoners were released from Fort Marion. Wohaw returned to his Kiowa Reservation, briefly attended school there but quit. He later joined an Indian Troop of the 7th Regiment of the U.S. Cavalry. After his discharge, he returned home again, this time to take an active part in the Ghost Dance religion, a visionary movement sweeping the Great Plains in the late 1880s that promised the end of white culture and the return of the buffalo. Wohaw died in 1924 on the Kiowa Reservation.

Perhaps it is no accident that Suzie Peters, field matron at the Anadarko, Oklahoma, Agency discovered five young Kiowa boys—Monroe Tsatoke, Stephen Mopope, James Auchiah, Jack Hokeah, and Spencer Asah—painting passionately with paper and watercolors borrowed from the Indian school. In 1918, she took some of the early drawings to Taos, New Mexico, and sold some to a dealer. Peters got the budding artists admitted to a mission school in Anadarko where Father Aloysius Hitta promised to help them become artists. By this time, Oscar Jacobson, head of the University of Oklahoma School of Art, knew about the young painters and invited them to live in Norman and paint at the university where he could keep track of them. Four of them went in 1927. (James Auchiah and Louise Smokey, the only woman in the group of painters, went later. Smokey was part of the group but apparently not counted since she would have made it the Kiowa Six.) Jacobson gave the artists a room at the art department where they could paint in privacy. The Kiowa painted each day, improving their skills in composition and proper anatomical proportions of people and horses. Jacobson encouraged them to develop their highly individual styles and urged them not to copy each other's style or the works of non-Indian students.

Within a few weeks of arriving at the university, the Kiowa exhibited their works in the art department. Within a few months, they produced enough paintings for a show in Denver at the American Federation of Arts Convention. In 1928, their paintings were sent to an international art festival in Prague, Czechoslovakia. Eventually, some of their works were exhibited at the Exposition of Indian Intertribal Arts in New York in 1930 where thousands of non-Indians saw Indian art for the first time.

In the late 1920s, Stephen Mopope, Spencer Asah, James Auchiah, and Jack Hokeah decorated the walls of the chapel of St. Patrick's Mission in Anadarko. During the early 1930s, the Kiowa painted murals before federal programs like the Works Progress Administration commissioned them to do works for public buildings. In 1930, Mopope and Hokeah painted murals at the University of Oklahoma. Asah and other Indians painted a mural for the school gymnasium at the Fort Sill Indian School; this mural is now covered by a heavy coat of paint. James Auchiah painted a 8 × 50 foot mural of the Harvest Dance for the Department of the Interior building in Washington, D.C.

With some practice, it is possible to pick out examples of the "Kiowa School" of painting, as these artists came to be known. Bold, flat colors, clear outlines, curviness, strong contrasts, no shading, no background scenery, and firm lines that separate color areas characterize the Kiowa style of painting. The Kiowa painters depicted realistic scenes of Plains Indian dance figures in tribal regalia, warfare, buffalo hunting, horses, and so on. The content echoes Plains Indian pictographic painting on animal hide and the drawings of Wohaw and the other prisoners at Fort Marion. The individual visions of Auchiah, Asah, Hokeah, Mopope, and Tsatoke expressed tribal tradition in new ways, however. These new ways of painting went on to influence other Indian painters in Oklahoma and generations of Indian painters in the Southwest as well. Doll artist Rhonda Holy Bear and painters Oscar Howe and Jaune Quick-to-See Smith, all of whom studied ledger art, credit its importance in the development of their artistic styles.

MARIA MARTINEZ

◆ ◆ ◆

San Ildefonso Potter
(c. 1885 – 1980)

I said to myself, "When I make pottery maybe I would help old people." That's my idea all the time. I'm not a dress woman, fix up myself; . . . I work, work . . . my Mother Earth gave me this luck. So I'm not going to keep it. I take care of our people.
— Maria Martinez, in *Maria* (1979)

Maria Montoya Martinez was born in the Tewa-speaking pueblo of San Ildefonso some time in the 1880s and died there a century later, perhaps the most famous Native American artist of all time. It was a century of dramatic change for the Pueblo Indians, and Maria was instrumental in helping her people incorporate radically new elements into their traditional ways both in the art and life of the community.

As the name of the pueblo and the potter indicate, Spanish influence was strong when Maria was born. The Spaniards had invaded the Southwest in the 16th century and their influence was pervasive. They brought horses and firearms, commercially made fabrics, containers and cooking utensils, their language and names, and their Roman Catholic religion. Much had been long absorbed into Pueblo life. The church was a part of the community just as their own kiva (Pueblo ceremonial chamber) was. The Tewa of San Ildefonso Pueblo celebrated Christmas and Saint Alfonso's day with traditional dances and ceremony and wore their rosaries as part of their regalia for traditional ceremonies. Though the pueblo is commonly known as San Ildefonso, it has a Tewa name, *P'owo'ge,* or "place where the waters meet." The village is on the upper Rio Grande near where it meets the Chama River, about 20 miles northwest of Santa Fe, or "Sacred Faith." The little girl baptized Maria Antonia Montoya, (Martinez was her married name) was also named *Poh've'ka,* which means "pond lily" in English. And when Maria married Julian Martinez, she had both a traditional Tewa ceremony and a Catholic ceremony. Maria was the second of five daughters. Though her parents always lived in San Ildefonso and Tewa was their first language, both knew Spanish and their daughters grew up bilingual. The family had Spanish friends and Maria played with Spanish as well as Tewa children as a young girl.

Maria was a good and happy girl, who enjoyed helping her mother. When her mother made cheese, Maria enjoyed selling and trading for it. She thought she might have a trading post or store when she grew up. Maria played with dolls and built a playhouse every year. When she needed dishes for her playhouse, Maria went to her Tia (aunt) Nicolasa, a skilled potter, for help. Every day Maria went and watched and finally she made a jar her aunt agreed to help her fire. As always, Tia Nicolasa sprinkled corn meal and said a prayer for the firing. Maria proudly gave her first jar to her mother as a present.

Maria went to the government school in the pueblo and then spent two years at St. Catherine's Indian School in Santa Fe. Maria always enjoyed working with her hands and at St. Catherine's she won her first prize—for sewing.

After Maria returned home to her pueblo, she met Julian Martinez, whom she had known as a bad and wild little boy. But they had both grown up. They fell in love and, in 1904, married. Life was hard and immediately after the wedding, Maria and Julian, along with other Pueblo Indians, went to the world's fair in St. Louis to earn money. There they danced and sang to entertain the crowds, and Maria made small bowls to sell.

After they returned home, Maria expected to settle down and begin her life as a traditional Tewa wife and mother. She had no artistic ambition. But life on the pueblo was changing. Since the building of the railroad in 1880, more and more Anglo-Americans were coming to the Southwest. Trees on the hills above the pueblo were cut down for lumber and, with the loss of the watershed, the waters flooded and destroyed the irrigation ditches and pueblo crops. Life was hard, food was scarce, and Maria had little time for pottery except for her own kitchen needs.

Beginning in 1907, Dr. Edgar Lee Hewett, an archaeologist and director of the Museum of New Mexico came to excavate and research old pueblo ruins near San Ildefonso. Julian began to work at the dig each summer. He was a good, hard worker, personable, always joking and well liked by the archaeologists. He began learning English and helped teach Tewa to the archaeologists who were interested. He discovered he could draw and draw well. He did the artwork for the dig, copying the pictures that were on the cave walls. He enjoyed drawing all sorts of his own pictures, too.

Maria didn't know it, but this excavation was going to change her life and the life at San Ildefonso. Among the ruins and artifacts, they dug up polishing stones and potsherds. Maria became interested. The polishing stones were wonderful, different colors, sizes and shapes, and they all "fit" Maria's hand perfectly. They had been used for smoothing and polishing the surfaces of clay pots. The shards were unlike anything Maria had seen, very beautiful and with a fine painted design. Since Maria was a fast and skillful potter and Julian's wife, Dr. Hewett asked if she would make a whole pot similar to the pot one of these shards might have come from. Julian could paint it.

Maria studied the shard, so thin and shiny, and saw that there was very fine sand in it, much finer than she was used to. She got the finest sand she could find and sifted it through cloth so she had only the finest grains. Then she did the same with her clay. It was more work than usual to prepare her clay, but when Maria began to build her bowl, it was velvety to touch and easy to handle. Her bowl grew quickly and polished easily with the treasured stones. It was perfectly round and thinner and smoother than any pot Maria had ever made.

Maria made her pottery the same way as Nampeyo did—by

pinching and coiling, smoothing and polishing—the method of their ancestors. When it was ready, the pot had to be painted the old way, too, for the archaeologist's experiment. Julian got some "guaco" for painting the design. Guaco is a native spinach that can be boiled down, painted on pottery, and fired into a black design. Julian also made his own paintbrush. He cut a blade from the leaf of a yucca plant and chewed off the thick part at one end so all that was left was the stringy fibre brush. Then he began to paint his black design on the light-colored pottery.

Julian was a natural abstract painter. To abstract means to take out, or separate, and an abstract artist takes out, or "abstracts," some elements of what he or she sees and uses that to restructure a new and different reality. When Julian plowed he saw the patterns in the furrows he made, and when he painted he abstracted the patterns he saw in things. For example, scalloped lines could be clouds, and a pattern of squares, the pueblo. Julian developed two designs that became so popular and copied that they almost symbolize the Southwest and Native American pottery. One design was an abstract eagle feather pattern that could radiate out from the center of a plate or form a band around a bowl or jar. The other was the "avanyu," or horned water serpent, which waved around a pot or plate. The waves for Julian were also waves of flowing water and the tongue, lightning—a symbol of thanks for rain and water.

The archaeologists were impressed with the pot. They now saw that perfectly round pottery could be made without a potter's wheel and fired on the ground without a kiln (oven). Dr. Hewett encouraged Maria and Julian and they began selling pottery at the museum in Santa Fe—the same museum that housed the artifacts from the dig. Shopkeepers bought them for their shops. The demand became so great that Maria began selling pots made by her sisters.

These early pieces of pottery by Maria and Julian were multi-colored. But some of the shards discovered on the excavation were shiny black all over. Could Maria and Julian make pottery like that? Maria and Julian knew that if pots were placed on the edge of the mound, or if there was a breeze during firing, the pots would get black smoke stains, but they weren't sure how to get the pots shiny and black all over. Julian had the mind of an inventor. He thought that if black stains were caused by smoke, smoke all over would make the pots black all over. The next firing Julian experimented. When the fire was burning hot enough, he threw on dry, powdery manure, creating a huge cloud of smoke. Julian smothered the fire without putting it out. When the pots came out they were black with a glossy sheen—like a black onyx stone.

The lustrous blackware was highly successful, and Julian had eliminated his painting job. But he experimented again. He began to paint with the wet polishing clay, or slip, on Maria's highly polished pottery and when it was fired they had a third style of pottery, one that became totally identified with Maria and Julian and San Ildefonso—black on black pottery. The pottery was made almost the same as before. Maria would burnish her pots, which she did better and faster than anyone, and Julian would paint his designs on top. When the fire was smothered the pots would come out black and lustrous where Maria had polished and dull and flat where Julian had painted.

The pottery business took off. People from New York, Boston, and Chicago ordered pottery. Maria and Julian opened a store where they sold pottery to the Anglos and groceries to the Spanish and Tewa. Maria had always cooked in her fireplace like other Tewa women. Now she bought a cast-iron stove, which she had enjoyed cooking on when she and Julian had lived and worked at the museum in Santa Fe. In 1924 they bought the first car in the pueblo; it was black and Julian painted it with his pottery designs. They became the drivers for the pueblo, helping anyone who needed a ride, and creating quite a sensation when they drove into Santa Fe.

Maria and Julian continued to refine their art. Maria built huge vessels with thin walls and a perfectly rounded, graceful shape and burnished them to a brilliant shine. When the Anglos suggested it, she developed a graceful plate form—which was not typical of the Pueblo Indians. Julian kept an ever growing notebook of designs, adding to it whenever he found something of interest. When he died in 1943, it was burned according to Tewa custom.

Maria Martinez of San Ildefonso Pueblo and Ralph T. Coe, curator, admiring Maria's pottery at the Nelson Gallery/Atkins Museum in Kansas City, Missouri, during the opening of the exhibit "Sacred Circles: 2,000 Years of North American Indian Art" in 1977. (Photography by M. de Montano)

But whatever success they had, Maria and Julian saw it as belonging to the pueblo of which they were a part. Unlike Euroamerican and Asian artists, they did not keep their methods and techniques secret. Maria and Julian shared their success with all the potters of San Ildefonso. They showed everyone how to fire black on blackware. They did not want to have more than other people had; that was not their way.

Maria and Julian traveled widely. They went to world's fairs in Chicago and San Francisco and to Indian powwows in Oklahoma. When traveling to a tribal expo in Alabama, they collected clay from 17 states they visited. Maria made pots from the clay of each state, and Julian painted each with a different design that symbolized for him the different states.

Maria was the first Pueblo potter to sign her pots. As the demand for her pots increased, Anglos suggested that she sign them and Maria obliged. But a signature does not always mean a "Maria" pot in the Anglo-European sense. The pots could be made in full or part by Maria, her sisters or other relatives. The painting was always done by Julian or other relatives. Pottery making was not an individual but a group effort and to Maria "authenticity" meant it was San Ildefonso pottery—that was what mattered. Maria sometimes signed pots for other Pueblo potters, and when Anglos brought her pots that they hoped were Maria's and asked her to sign, she obliged even if they were not hers.

When Julian died in 1943, Maria continued making pottery for another 30 years, and other family members helped with the painting. Maria also taught pottery not only to the other women in her pueblo, but to others at the Indian School in Santa Fe and, when she was an old woman, at the Idyllwild School of Music and Art in California.

Maria Martinez received endless awards and honors. She won several prizes at the Indian fairs in Santa Fe and Gallup, various New Mexican awards and citations and honors from many museums and national organizations. She received the Craftsmanship Medallion from the American Institute of Architects, the nation's highest honor for craftspeople, and in 1954 the Palmes Académiques from the French government for her outstanding contribution to the field of art. Several honorary doctorates amused her. As she put it, "I don't want to be a doctor! I never medicate anyone!" Maria met with world-renowned European and Japanese potters. She traveled to New York City and laid the cornerstone at Rockefeller Center. She visited the White House several times.

Maria Martinez comfortably merged the two worlds in which she lived. She dined in the White House with Eleanor Roosevelt and Lady Bird Johnson but lived all her life in a simple San Ildefonso home. She made lots of money, which she invested in her village and helping others, not in stocks and bonds. She especially loved Eleanor Roosevelt who said to her, "Keep the Indian way. Send your children to school but keep your own way."

Maria was also blessed with remarkable strength of character. It enabled her to remain true to herself as a Tewa woman. In spite of her achievements she was modest and never over-whelmed by material success. She persisted and sustained her sense of self and purpose in the face of much personal tragedy. Her husband Julian became an alcoholic and Maria cared for him until he died. Several children died in infancy, including a daughter also named Pond Lily, and three of her four adult sons died before she did. When Maria was a young mother, her own mother died in childbirth and Maria brought up her baby sister Clara as her own child. She was never bitter. Maria Martinez had a happy and serene disposition and tremendous generosity of spirit. She could derive as much pleasure from simple things and beauty as from her tremendous achievements. Perhaps her greatest satisfaction came from what she did for others, the eco-nomic sustenance she was able to give to her pueblo, the pleasure of pottery she was able to share with others, and the generosity and help she was able to offer others because of her success. Maria Martinez died in 1980 in San Ildefonso Pueblo.

ALLAN HOUSER

◆ ◆ ◆

Chiricahua Apache Sculptor
(1914 – 94)

What I'm trying to do is portray the Indian in a beautiful way,
and in a very contemporary way. I want to emphasize
something that for years and years people just took for granted
and ignored. The Indians were here. So what. Well, I am trying
to change that.
—Allan Houser, in *Allan Houser of (Ha-o-zous)* (1987)

Allan Haozous (an Apache word meaning "the sound of pulling
roots"), a Chiricahua Apache, was born June 30, 1914 on a family
farm in Boone, Oklahoma, near Apache, Oklahoma. His mother,
Blossom, the half-Apache daughter of George Wratten, superintendent of the Apache at Fort Sill, was born in captivity at a military
post in Alabama. His father, Sam Haozous, the grandson of the
legendary chief Mangas Coloradas, fought with Geronimo as a
young boy. Geronimo, the fiercely independent Chiricahua
Apache leader, and his band of Apache tried to resist whites who
had invaded their Arizona homelands. Defeated by the U.S. Army
in 1886, they were taken prisoner, and Sam, a teenager, spent the
next 27 years in captivity in Fort Marion, Florida, and Fort Sill,
Oklahoma before being freed in 1913.

After he was released, Sam and the other surviving members of
the band were directed to either go live on an Apache reservation
in New Mexico or take a 160-acre farming allotment of land near

Apache, Oklahoma. Sam and Blossom chose Oklahoma and farming, which was a hard way to make a living, especially later during the Depression years. Despite their struggles with floods, dust, hail, drought, tornadoes, sickness, and poverty, Sam and Blossom raised their five children to feed the hungry, shelter the homeless, and honor all people. As Allan later recalled, "That's how we were raised. I learned to respect all human beings, all colors of skin. Dad said, 'They are people just like you and me.'"

Sam and Blossom gave Allan and his siblings even more. They gave the children a solid pride in their Apache cultural identity. Houser still misses those nights when his father and mother told them old stories or sang in Apache. Their stories explained the creation of day and night, birds and animals, especially wily coyote (see p. 119 for an explanation of coyote stories), and Apache rituals. Sam retold stories about fighting with Geronimo, about the old days when Apache were free, and the anguish of captivity. Sam sang Geronimo's war songs, accompanying himself with an Apache drum, and Blossom joined in. Many years later, Houser preserved his parents' stories about Apache culture in his paintings and monumental sculptures.

As a youth, Allan worked hard on the family farm, and his schooling was interrupted when he had to work in the cotton fields or carry cold water to workers harvesting wheat. At first, schooling was difficult for Allan because he spoke Apache, not English. Allan suffered because classmates had trouble pronouncing his last name, so he changed it to Houser. He completed grade school in 1928 at Boone Public School and that year went off to Chilocco Indian boarding school in northern Oklahoma. In 1929, Allan's father needed help on the farm so Allan's high school education ended for the time being.

School had never suited Allan anyway. He drew when he should have been studying. In the evenings, after farm work, Allan found time to draw. His father advised him about the details of traditional Apache clothing and equipment. Longing to go to art school, even though his parents wanted him to raise cattle for a living, Allan was accepted at Santa Fe Indian School in the fall of 1934.

The school was the only place in the United States where Allan could get a decent education without a high-school diploma. There, he studied with Dorothy Dunn, the founder of the school's art program called the Studio (see pp. 39–40 for discussion of Dunn's Studio). Drawing on his father's stories, he painted scenes of traditional Apache life—religious and social dances, buffalo hunts, burials, horses and riders, wildlife—in the flat, two-dimensional decorative style that the school's Studio encouraged.

If students objected, they were told to leave. Although Allan credits Dunn for giving him the basics and getting him started, he felt stifled by Dunn, who "protected" them from knowing anything about non-Indian art movements and discouraged them from painting with light and shadow. Disappointed by Dunn who told him, "Allan, I don't like what you are doing at all," he reacted with "That's too bad because I do." In 1936, after Allan earned the Studio's Arts and Crafts award, he told his parents he wanted to become an artist. It took years, however, before he broke away from the style that earned him the school's recognition. In 1937, Houser had his first one-man show of 19 watercolor paintings at the Museum of Fine Arts in Santa Fe; in that same year, he was the only Indian represented in the National Exhibition of American Art in New York City.

In 1938, Houser and a painter friend opened a studio in Santa Fe, but "darn near starved to death" before they were saved in 1939 by an invitation to paint murals inside the Interior Department building in Washington, D.C. More invitations to paint murals followed: the 1939 Golden Gate Exposition in San Francisco and the New York World's Fair; 11 years later, he did dioramas for the Southern Plains Indian Museum in Anadarko, Oklahoma. In 1940, when Houser was studying mural techniques with Olle Nordmark, a Swedish artist who taught at the Fort Sill Indian Art Center, the instructor noticed a sculptural quality in Houser's drawings. Nordmark suggested he give sculpture a try, but it was decades before Houser turned to that career full time.

During World War II, Houser struggled to support his wife, Anna Marie, and four children in Los Angeles where he took a job as a pipe fitter's helper in a synthetic rubber plant. At night, he studied art books, spent hours investigating new art movements in museums and galleries, drew, watercolored, and carved wood. In his spare time, he wandered around Otis Art Institute studying the sculpture. Luckily, a sculpture teacher got him interested in stone, told him what tools he needed, and got Houser started. In 1948, with no experience, he entered a sculpture competition sponsored by the Haskell Institute Alumni Association in Lawrence, Kansas. His design won first place.

Houser moved his family to Lawrence where he proceeded to make his first (and the nation's first Native American) public monument. *Comrade in Mourning*, standing 7½ feet tall and carved from almost five tons of Carrara marble, is a memorial to Indian servicemen who died during World War II. The work forecast Houser's direction: massive, textured surfaces, realistic faces and understated Native figures.

Shortly after he finished *Comrade in Mourning*, Houser won two Guggenheim Fellowships—in painting and sculpture. He and his family ended up on the Haozous family farm where he created art in a converted surplus barracks. After the fellowship ended, Houser started teaching, a career that lasted until he retired in 1975. During the 1950s, he taught painting and carving to Navajos at the Intermountain Indian School in Brigham City, Utah, often working 15 to 20 hours a day. His dedication to teaching won him international acclaim when, in 1956, the French government awarded him the Palmes Académique, the first of many awards that recognized his contributions as a teacher and artist.

In 1962, he joined the staff of the new Institute of American Indian Arts in Santa Fe, on the old Santa Fe Indian School campus. From the start, Houser impressed the students with his dignity and power and broadened their horizons about non-Indian art. He exposed them to modern painting and sculpture and walked them up mountains to get pieces of wood to carve in class. He ignored the criticism that he and the other instructors were traitors to their own traditions and the charge that they were making abstract artists out of the students. He told his students:

You're Indian youngsters, make the most of that, but don't feel you
have to do your art a certain way. Grow with the times. Don't forget
your heritage, and with it you can find enough material to be the
greatest artists in the world.

Under Houser's influence, a new generation of Native American
sculptors emerged and built successful careers, including his son
Bob Haozous, with whom he shared a two-man show in 1983 at
the Heard Museum in Phoenix, Arizona.

While Houser was teaching full time and taking college painting
and sculpture courses himself, he managed to pour out his own
paintings, drawings, stone and wood carvings, including his first
bronze casting in 1968. It was no accident that from the start
Houser honored the parents he admired as well as their teachings
through his art. Family, parenting, women, mother-and-child images, herders, storytellers, musicians, dancers, drummers, Apache
warriors and singers, animals, and other themes from the stories
his parents told him as a child made their way from memory into
carvings and paintings. By the time Houser retired as head of the
sculpture department at the Institute in 1975, after teaching 25
years, he was the leading Native American sculptor.

At 61 years of age, Houser began a new chapter in his life. He
turned to sculpture full time. He now spends long hours at his
studio near Santa Fe. Although he enjoys making bronze, wood,
and welded steel sculptures, it thrills him to work in stone. As
Houser described it,

> You pull it up out of the earth. It's almost alive . . . You see this
> sculpture in there and it's almost complete. The thrill is roughing
> out a stone and suddenly seeing a face or hand emerge. The stone
> comes to life.

A powerful hoist lifts enormous blocks of uncut stone off deliv-
ery trucks and swings them into position. Wearing earmuffs and
a respirator for indoor work, Houser sets to work with air
hammers, chisels, grinders, rasps, files, spatulas, and other carving tools, some of which he invented. With his cutting tools, and

the assistance of apprentices, he has turned blocks of Italian, Portuguese, or Vermont marble and Indiana limestone into heads or busts, full or partial single figures, circles of figures, or animals. Most of Houser's work until recently has been of figures, and from the beginning these figures have been drawn from Indian themes, especially Apache culture. He also uses Pueblo, Navajo, and other Plains Indian subjects because he has personal knowledge of these peoples. He emphasizes faces, heads, and hands and contrasts them with larger, generalized areas of smooth or rough surfaces. The figures may be holding a water pot or ceremonial drum. Size presents no problem for Houser who said, "Working in a larger scale, I can express myself much better."

Rarely does Houser create a piece with an element of sorrow. The figures are at peace, resting, praying, cradling a newborn, watching a dance, hunting, or journeying home (a favorite theme for Houser who grew up in Oklahoma but visits Apache reservations to stay in contact with the culture). Whatever figure Houser makes, he strives to convey his or her human dignity—"this dignity, this goodness that is in man. I hope I am getting it across. If I am, then I am doing what I have always wanted."

By the end of the 1970s, Houser's works were being shown all over the United States. Viewers might see *Storyteller* (1975) carved in alabaster depicting an Apache elder telling a story to three youngsters. Or they might have seen *Earth Song* (1978) a larger-than-life, 900-pound Vermont marble figure of an Apache drummer installed at the Heard Museum. In 1983, Houser's life-size, half-ton bronze *Chiricahua Apache Family* was unveiled at the Fort Sill Apache Tribal Center in Apache, Oklahoma. The sculpture honors the memory of his parents and commemorates the 70th anniversary of the release of Apache prisoners (Houser's parents among them) from Fort Sill. Two years later, *Offering of the Sacred Pipe*, a seven-foot-tall bronze figure offering a peace pipe skyward was dedicated in the courtyard of the United States mission to the United Nations in New York City.

Although many of Houser's sculptures have been of realistic figures, he is moving toward sculpture of increasing simplicity and abstraction. Generalized human forms have subtle clues that

Allan Houser working on Resting at the Spring, *a sculpture created from Indiana limestone, 94" x 45" x 24", in 1986.* (Photograph courtesy of Glenn Green Galleries, Santa Fe, New Mexico)

they are Native American. Birds created in abstract forms also give clues that suggest what they are. "Doing things that are not completely abstract, but semiabstract, is exciting—more exciting than doing strictly realistic work," according to Houser.

Besides sculpture, Houser's interest in music has led him to play the harmonica, the Indian flute, the guitar, Apache violin, mouth harp, and on occasion, the drum. Music helps him with his work: "You need a little break now and then. Often I come back to something I've been working on and see something very obvious I've been overlooking."

Houser's sculpture is in the permanent collections of major museums around the country. Besides numerous one-man shows, the 1983 retrospective he shared with his son, and a 1991 major retrospective at the Museum of Fine Arts in Santa Fe (54 years after his first one-man show there in 1937), a Houser exhibition toured Europe in 1983. Houser's sculpture is sold exclusively through the Glenn Green Galleries located in Santa Fe, New Mexico, and Scottsdale, Arizona. Houser, the subject of two documentary films, is also the subject of countless articles and books.

During his long career filled with constant acclaim, travel all over the world (especially to Italy to see first-hand where marble, a favorite material, comes from), and a 1979 artist-in-residence at Dartmouth College in New Hampshire, Houser has received honors too numerous to mention. In 1967, the Indian Arts and Crafts Board gave him a Certificate of Appreciation, in 1969 the Philbrook Art Center in Tulsa, Oklahoma, awarded him its coveted Waite Phillips Trophy, and in 1980, he received the New Mexico Governor's Award for the Visual Arts. Three years later he received the Oklahoma Governor's Visual Arts Award and, in 1985, entered the Oklahoma Hall of Fame. Besides the National Ethnic Medal and the Cowboy Hall of Fame's Prix de West, in 1992 President George Bush presented Houser with the National Medal of the Arts, a fitting tribute for one of the nation's greatest sculptors.

OSCAR HOWE

◆ ◆ ◆

Dakota Painter
(1915 –1983)

*One of my reasons for painting is to record visually and
artistically the culture of the American Indian, particularly
the Dakota Indian.*

—Oscar Howe,
from "Theories and Beliefs—Dakota," (1969)

Oscar Howe, (Mazuha Hokshina meaning "Trader Boy" in the
Dakota language), a member of the Yanktonai band of Dakota
(Sioux), was born on May 13, 1915 at Joe Creek on the Crow Creek
Indian Reservation in South Dakota. His parents were George Tikute
Howe and Ella Fearless Bear, both Yanktonai Dakota. He was de-
scended from a number of hereditary chiefs—his great-grandfathers
were Chief White Bear and Bone Necklace, head chief of the Lower
Yanktonai people who was an eloquent spokesman for his people
in the late 1800s. Howe's grandfathers were also chiefs.

Howe was sent to a Bureau of Indian Affairs boarding school
when he was seven years old; he was subjected to U.S. government
educational policies that tried to strip him and other Indian children of their cultural heritage and turn them into Euroamericans.
The boys' hair was cut. Their Native clothing was taken away and
replaced with Euroamerican garments. Their diet was changed.
After Oscar developed a skin disease, the open sores discouraged
children from coming near him, adding to the isolation he already

felt because he spoke Siouan and the other children talked in English. Only drawing comforted him.

He tried running away several times, and even contemplated killing himself as did other Indian children stuck in boarding schools at that time. Considered a hopeless case by school officials, Oscar was sent back to the Crow Creek Reservation and placed with Shell Face, his maternal grandmother who cared for him. His mother had died when Howe was nine. Under his grandmother's care, the body sores eventually healed. In the time Howe spent with Shell Face, she told him many stories about his Dakota heritage. Years later these stories provided Howe with the major subjects of his life's work in painting.

When Oscar was 11 years old, he returned to boarding school. He finished 8th grade when he was 18. In elementary school, Howe had showed promise, winning art contests. So, in 1935, when he was 20, the federal government sent Howe to the Santa Fe Indian School in New Mexico. This school became an important place in the preservation, revival, and marketing of Indian arts. Government policy makers, saw Indian art as a way for Indians to make money and as a skill that would enable them to continue their traditional lifestyles. Federal monies housed, fed, clothed, and provided supplies and equipment to Indian student artists.

The student artists attended painting classes in the Studio program started by the fine arts teacher Dorothy Dunn. Dunn directed them to be true to their tribal traditions. It has been reported she was careful not to pressure anyone into painting what their elders didn't want them to paint. She urged them, however, to follow certain painting rules. Dunn wanted them to stick to painting scenes they remembered from their reservations or Pueblo village life in color on white or neutral backgrounds with no spatial depth. She wanted them to paint formal compositions with flat clear figures, animals, or birds with lots of detail in opaque colors crisply outlined in black. She wanted students to use designs that only came from their own tribes.

The students either used their memories of tribal designs on pottery, baskets, or clothing, or Dunn provided books, drawings, and photographs for artistic inspiration. Howe and his peers, some of whom (such as Allan Houser, see chapter on Houser) became renowned artists, ended up being indoctrinated with the Studio rules. Some students balked at all the rules and did as they pleased. They crossed tribal lines. They used earth-derived colors, and they did not paint the subject matter Dunn wanted them to. But most of the students painted in the Studio style because that was the kind of Indian art the public wanted to buy. Howe graduated as salutatorian in 1938, one of the Studio's greatest successes, but it was years before he broke away from the painting style that Dunn's Studio encouraged.

Howe's early work, done in Studio style, reflected his childhood in which elders taught him ancient Dakota customs. He also worked in the traditional Dakota "point-and-line" rules, which Howe explained meant creating a design from point to point, with connecting lines either straight or curved. While continuing to develop as an artist, in 1939, Howe taught art at the Pierre Indian Boarding School. After he received offers to do mural art, he decided to train with Olle Nordmark, a leading muralist in Oklahoma until World War II interrupted his career.

After serving in Europe for three and a half years, where he painted camouflage on army equipment, Howe returned to the United States and to painting. In 1947, he was invited to enter the Second Annual American Indian Art competition sponsored by the Philbrook Art Center in Tulsa, Oklahoma, at that time the most important exhibition for Native Americans. His painting *Dakota Duck Hunt* won the Grand Purchase Prize, gave him great exposure to art buyers and museums, and provided funds that enabled him to send for and marry Heidi Hampel, a woman he had met overseas duing the war.

In 1948, Howe became Artist-in-Residence at Dakota Wesleyan University in Mitchell, South Dakota. Here he also received his undergraduate degree and was appointed acting chairman of the school's art department during his senior year. He received a Master of Fine Arts degree from the University of Oklahoma in 1954. In 1957 he was appointed assistant professor of fine arts at the University of South Dakota in Vermillion, where he remained until he retired in 1980.

By the time Howe graduated in 1954, he was beginning to combine his Studio experiences with the lessons he learned about modern painting. After he moved to the University of South Dakota in 1957, Howe's artistic style emerged—a style that revolutionized Indian art, broke the rules that had limited the creativity of Indian artists for years, changed the course of art history, and inspired other Indian artists to do the same. "Without Oscar Howe and his introduction of a new approach," wrote one art critic, "Native American painters would quite probably still be trying to overcome restrictive rules imposed by the non-Indian world."

One of Howe's greatest contributions was challenging the often-asked question "Does he paint like an Indian?" In 1958, Howe submitted a painting of a war and peace dance with complex linear patterns to the Philbrook Art Annual. The jury, which included Indian artists, judged painting by a set of rules prescribing what Indian painting should look like—no perspective, no shading, recognizable Indian subjects, and other requirements that reflected Studio definitions. Howe was furious after the jury rejected his painting as being "a fine painting—but not Indian." On April 18, 1958 he protested in a letter to Jeanne O. Snodgrass, curator of Indian art at the Philbrook:

> Who ever said that my paintings are not in the traditional Indian style has poor knowledge of Indian art indeed. There is much more to Indian art than pretty, stylized pictures . . . . Are we to be held back forever with one phase of Indian painting, with no right for individualism, dictated to as the Indian always has been, put on reservations and treated like a child, and only the White Man knows what is best for him? Now, even in Art, "You little child do what we think is best for you, nothing different." Well, I am not going to stand for it.

Howe convinced the Philbrook jury and the next year the rules for eligibility were changed. Four years later, in 1963, Howe won the Philbrook Grand Purchase Award for *Hehakawinyan—Elk Woman*. This painting, with its circular composition and rhythmic movement, never would have made it into competition if Howe had not told the Philbrook "I am not going to stand for it." Thanks to Howe's protest, he and other painters today are free to express themselves as they please. Other galleries as well have changed their rules and admitted almost every aspect of art, from the traditional to the modern.

By the late 1950s, Howe began creating paintings derived from his Dakota heritage. The stories that Shell Face had told him as a youth about Dakota rituals, especially tribal dances, filled the canvases. So did images from Dakota traditional stories such as the birth of the first Dakota people and animals and nature.

On occasion an event in tribal history, such as the Wounded Knee Massacre, would turn up on a canvas. On December 29, 1890, in the midst of negotiations between Colonel James William Forsyth, commander of the U.S. 7th Cavalry, and the Lakota encamped at Wounded Knee, South Dakota, an unknown person fired a shot and the army opened fire with Hotchkiss guns and mowed down some 300 Lakota people, almost all women, children, and elderly.

Although Howe was aware of his people's unjust treatment, with the exception of Wounded Knee paintings, he avoided painting the horrible things that happened to Indians. He preferred doing paintings that celebrated the richness of his culture. In 1970, he summed up his approach: "One of my reasons for painting is to record visually and artistically the culture of the American Indian, particularly the Dakota Indian." He also stated that another reason for his painting was "to carry on what is traditional and conventional in art. It is a custom in Dakota culture to be a contributing member as to your talent and need." The Dakota people traditionally recorded tribal history and individual exploits on dried hides of buffalos (discussed on pages 17–18). Howe painted with casein (which resembles tempera—water, glue, and egg base) used by Dakota for some of their hide paintings.

Howe also painted subject matter similar to that found on hide paintings, but he merged it with an artistic style that has been called cubism (geometric forms used in many combinations). Howe, while aware of cubism, denied that his mature works were influenced by European cubist painting styles. He maintained that his style grew from traditional Plains Indian art and that Dakota

Oscar Howe, a Dakota artist, in his studio around 1974. (Photograph courtesy of The University Art Galleries, University of South Dakota)

always used abstract or geometric forms in many combinations. He said he did not learn anything about cubism when he was stationed in Europe during World War II because he was restricted to an army base. After he returned to the United States, he went to South Dakota, equally isolated in terms of learning about cubism.

Howe painted in an abstract style, where human figures, animals, and landscape appear in complex linear patterns. Howe credited nature for his paintings that literally explode with lines. In 1969, Howe wrote: "Movements in nature such as sun, earth, rainfall, lightning, growth, flight, fire, arrow, rays of light, eye movements are straight smooth movements; sounds and sights all emphasized with the straight line." Howe started making those remarkable lines into abstract drawings when he was only three years old. He remembered:

such drawings were complete abstractions and not Indian abstract symbols nor recognizable objects. I thought my first lines were beautiful, plastic, and full of tension; . . . I remember my parents saw these lines and told me to never draw again. I still made those lines when no one was watching. . . . Eventually I came in contact with other children who drew recognizable objects. I drew objects too, but I always managed to keep my drawings more linear.

Howe's paintings also explode with colors that he felt might have come from his subconscious knowledge of the meanings of color in Dakota culture. He knew yellow was the Dakota color for religion; red meant fire or blood; blue, peace; green, growth; white, purity; and black, evil. He used these colors in symbolic ways. In *Origin of the Sioux,* which depicts the story of the birth of the first Dakota, he used yellow to create a spiritual mood. Howe acknowledged that meanings of colors differed among Indian groups, and he felt artists were free to use color for personal reasons.

In 1974, Howe suffered a severe heart attack, but he continued to work. However, he became ill with Parkinson's disease, an incapacitating condition, and eventually could no longer paint. He died October 7, 1983 in the Southeastern Dakota Nursing Home in Vermillion, South Dakota.

The University of South Dakota at Vermillion owns the largest collection of Howe's works and maintains a gallery with permanent displays of his paintings. The Howe Art Center in Mitchell, South Dakota, maintains a gallery with about 20 of his paintings. In 1982, these two institutions organized the first major retrospective of his paintings. Some 100 works toured five U.S. locations.

Before he died, Howe won numerous awards at national art competitions and exhibitions and he also received three honorary doctorates from institutions, 15 gold medals and first place awards, plus the title of Artist Laureate of South Dakota. He was the first recipient of the South Dakota's Governor's Award for Creative Achievement. Perhaps, most fitting, the Philbrook Art Center, which once rejected one of his paintings, in 1966 awarded him its coveted Waite Phillips Trophy for his outstanding career.

HELEN CORDERO

◆ ◆ ◆

Cochiti Storyteller Dollmaker
(1915 – ⁹⁰)

I don't know why people go for my work the way they do.
Maybe it's because to me they aren't just pretty things that I
make for money. All my potteries come out of my heart.
They're my little people. I talk to them and they're singing. If
you're listening, you can hear them.
— Helen Cordero, from *The Pueblo Storyteller* (1986)

Helen Cordero was born on June 17, 1915 in Cochiti Pueblo, New
Mexico, a village south of Santa Fe, New Mexico, that was settled
around 1250 on the Rio Grande. She grew up in the pueblo (the
Spanish word for village), one of 19 pueblos located in New
Mexico. Since ancient times, people in these pueblos have made
objects out of clay. At Cochiti Pueblo women shaped clay vessels
to store water, grains, and corn and made small clay figures of
women as well as animals and birds in their environment. The
women created some of the figurines as toys for their children but
most were used in religious ceremonies. During the 16th century,
the Spanish clergy interrupted the tradition because they believed
the figures were heathen images. Spanish priests smashed all the
clay figures they could find and tried to prevent the potters from
making new ones. Despite this harrassment, women in the pueblos
continued to make clay figures. In the late 1800s, almost all the
potters in the Rio Grande pueblos made some human or animal

clay figures, but the quality and quantity declined. Helen's pueblo of Cochiti led the others in producing exotic figurines that Indian traders snapped up and then sold to tourists. About the time Helen was born, only a few Cochiti women were still making a small pottery figure of a woman with a child, referred to as a "singing mother," and figures of Pueblo drummers and dancers. Helen Cordero calls it a time when "pottery was silent in the pueblo."

Helen Cordero grew up speaking fluently in the three languages of the Rio Grande region—Keresan, Spanish, and English—married Fred Cordero, a painter and one of Cochiti's finest drum makers, and raised six children. In the late 1950s, Helen, surrounded by artists and eager to express her own creativity plus make a little extra money, tried her hand at leather-working and beadwork with Juanita Arquero, her husband's cousin. Most of the money Helen and her cousin made, however, went right back into buying materials. When Fred Cordero's aunt suggested that the women start making pottery, reminding them "You don't have to buy anything; Mother Earth gives it all to you," Helen Cordero spent six months studying with Arquero who had learned the ancient art of making pottery as a child.

Since Cordero's bowls and jars kept coming out crooked and never looked right, Arquero suggested that Cordero make figures instead and "it was like a flower blooming." Cordero spent several years making countless tiny figures of birds, animals, and eventually "little people." Cordero's husband painted details on the figures until she was confident enough to paint them herself.

In 1960, when Cordero showed some of her figures at Santo Domingo feast day, the renowned folk art collector Alexander Girard bought all the "little people" (male and female figures standing eight to nine inches high) for $7.50 each and encouraged her to make more figures and to make them larger. Besides commissioning her to make a 250-piece Nativity set, he asked her to make a large seated figure with many children, similar to the "singing mothers" which Cordero and other Cochiti potters made.

Cordero recalled going home and thinking about her grandfather, Santiago Quintana: "I kept seeing my grandfather. That one, he was a really good storyteller and there were always lots of us grandchildren around him." Cordero, like other children in the pueblos, was raised in a tradition where storytelling was a regular event after the evening meal during long winter nights when the earth, plants, animals, and people were quiet and resting. Many stories were told only during winter because people were safe from hibernating snakes and lightning. Children gathered around an elder, usually a man, who told stories. These were stories that he had heard from his grandfather, who had heard the exact same stories from his grandfather. The elders' stories recounted the creation of the world, people, plants, animals, birds, and fish; the correct way to behave; the history of Cochiti; or elders might even tell some personal story or give a prophecy. Cordero's grandfather, who was one of Cochiti Pueblo's gifted storytellers, also befriended many anthropologists and other people who observed Pueblo life. He wanted to preserve the traditions of his people and make sure the scholars "got it right." So for more than 40 years, beginning in the late 1800s, he shared information about Cochiti culture, retold traditional stories, and took anthropologists on trips to canyons.

In 1964, Cordero remembered her grandfather's voice when she made her first storyteller doll. That doll turned out to be an eight-inch high Pueblo grandfather figure, Santiago, telling stories to five grandchildren, three perched on his shoulders and two sitting on his lap. By making the figure male instead of female, she changed the "singing mothers" tradition. And by placing five children on the figure, she launched the new tradition of placing numbers of children on the figures. Storyteller dolls now have as many as 30 boys and girls attached to them. In her first doll, Cordero painted open eyes on her grandfather storyteller, but after that she made her figures with closed eyes and open mouths explaining: "His eyes are closed because he's thinking and his mouth is open because he's telling stories."

Cordero's dolls were immediately popular and successful. In 1964, the year she made her very first storyteller doll, she carried off first, second, and third prizes at the New Mexico State Fair. Cordero believed her success was due to the fact that she made her dolls "the right way, the old way."

Cordero didn't buy her clay or paints like other potters. Nature provided her art materials. She gathered different types of clay on or near the reservation and pounded, sifted, mixed, and kneaded them the way Cochiti potters did hundreds of years before her. To make black paint, she gathered the guaco plant (also called wild spinach or Rocky Mountain bee plant) that grows wild in New Mexico. After boiling it into a sludge and allowing it to harden into a cake, it became the basis for black paint, or guaco, that could be used like watercolor paint. She collected red earth that she turned into terra-cotta-colored paint.

For the overall surface color of her dolls, Cordero coated them with a thin wash of gray clay and water before firing them in her yard. Sometimes she reapplied more coats of the gray wash and refired the pieces until the surface color pleased her. Cordero did use modern technology when it served her needs. She painted her facial expressions and clothing details with camel hair brushes rather than yucca brushes, and she smoothed her figures with sandpaper rather than polishing stones because it was easier to get into the crevices around the numerous children.

At first, Cordero pulled the children out of the primary piece of clay. Gradually, she began to make the children separately and attach them to the storyteller, which she made taller, thinner, and better proportioned. In addition to her trademark faces—which have closed eyes, open mouths, and heads tilted back—since 1970, she has printed her name and "Cochiti Pueblo" in guaco on the bottom of her pieces. The pieces she made in the 1960s were either unsigned or signed in script in pencil or pen after she fired them.

Cordero has lost track of the number of dolls she has made since that first one in 1964, explaining that making her dolls was like making bread. "We don't count." No two dolls are alike, however. They range in height from seven to 16 inches, with anywhere from three to 30 children on each storyteller, all with different body positions. Whatever the number of children, she painted different facial expressions and clothing details with two colors, black and terra cotta (reddish brown). She might give the storyteller braids or long and free-flowing hair, short cuts, or chongos (knotted style). The grandfather wears either a hat or headband or nothing, and she painted shirts with flowers, stripes, plaids, embroidery, ribbons, or traditional Cochiti pottery designs. Or she painted the shirt plain white, terra cotta (reddish brown), or black. Children scamper over their elders, cling and hug each other, snuggle into laps or sit alert on their storytellers. Some sleep while others smile. Sometimes puppies nestle among the children.

Helen was so successful with her storyteller dolls that she produced other images from her family and Pueblo experiences. Besides making Nativity scenes, she has shaped Pueblo fathers, Cochiti ceremonial figures, owls, and turtles. She also made a drummer, a popular figure that other Cochiti potters had been making since the 1950s. Cochiti men are famous among the other pueblos for making fine drums that are used in ceremonies, sold to other pueblos for ceremonial use, or sold to Anglos who use them as decoration. Cordero modeled her drummer after her husband, Fred, who was a well-known drummer, drum maker, and several times governor of Cochiti Pueblo.

In addition to making drummers, other Pueblo figures, and animals, Cordero experimented with her own storyteller invention. In 1971, she grouped five separate children near the storyteller figure, rather than attaching them to him. She called this new version *The Children's Hour* and explained that "These are older children listening to him. My grandpa used to say 'Come children, it's time,' and I remember us all around him out at the ranch in the summer, and that's how I thought of the Children's Hour." The first time she showed her new version, it won a blue ribbon at the Phoenix Heard Museum's Indian Arts and Crafts Show. In another variation on her storyteller figures, in the mid-1970s, she made a praying storyteller, in which the adult figure kneels rather than sits and the children scramble over his legs behind him. According to Helen, she made it that way because an art collector got down on his hands and knees and begged her for a storyteller, threatening to stay there until she made him one. In 1984, she created what she called her Navajo storyteller. Instead of putting the children on a grandfather figure with legs, she placed the children on the apron of the storyteller, now a grandmother figure.

Helen Cordero has won more prizes than she can count. The

recognition began in 1964, the year she entered her first major competition at the New Mexico State Fair and walked off with first, second, and third prizes. A year later she took all three awards at the important Santa Fe Indian Market. In 1968, she took first prize at the Phoenix, Arizona, Heard Museum First Annual Indian Arts and Crafts Exhibit, and she took prizes again in 1969. In 1970, after her Nativity scene won "Best of Show," the Heard purchased it for its permanent collection and has exhibited it every Christmas since. In 1971, a storyteller doll took first prize in the "Traditional Pottery, Painted, Miscellaneous" category at Indian Market. By 1980, there was a category for "storytellers," a sure sign that clay figures were considered an art form by art collectors and dealers. Her first one-person show in Scottsdale, Arizona, in 1973 was sold out before it began. Cordero has given pottery-making demonstrations from Pecos National Monument in New Mexico to Kent State University in Ohio. Her dolls have been included in national and international exhibitions, and in 1981–82, the Wheelwright Museum in Santa Fe, New Mexico, mounted a major retrospective of her work. After one of Cordero's dolls was featured on the cover of *Sunset Magazine*, the demand for her work increased with orders piling up from around the nation. In 1982, Helen received one of the New Mexico Governor's Awards for Excellence and Achievements in the Arts. In 1986, the Folk Arts Program of the National Endowment for the Arts honored her for her contributions to America's cultural heritage.

When Helen Cordero invented her first storyteller doll in 1964, she had no idea that her success would set off an incredible revival of the tradition of making pottery figures. She had, of course, reinvented the long-standing tradition of making pottery figures that existed in her own and other pueblos before Spanish priests tried to stop their production. Cordero's blue ribbons, popularity, and financial success stimulated other women in Cochiti Pueblo to make storyteller dolls. By the mid-1980s, some 20 years after Cordero made her first piece, at least 55 Cochiti potters, including members of Cordero's own family, were making clay figures, many winning prizes. But it didn't stop at Cochiti. Cordero's dolls influenced potters in other New Mexico pueblos as well. Today,

Helen Cordero of Cochiti Pueblo making one of her storyteller dolls. (Photo by Dudley Smith, 1979. Photograph courtesy of: Photo Archives, Denver Museum of Natural History, all rights reserved)

more than 200 potters make storyteller dolls in all shapes and sizes, including animal storytellers first created by Acoma and Cochiti potters, using local clays, paints, and designs. These potters, who also had grandparents or elders who told them stories, had found a way to celebrate their storytelling traditions.

Helen Cordero has had mixed feelings about the success of storyteller dolls. Even though she has been pleased that her work inspired others and "really started something" and even though she has been aware that she revived the tradition of Pueblo clay figures, Cordero has not always liked the countless reproductions of something that was for her a personal memory of her grandfather. She has seen her storyteller "invention" used on notecards, Christmas cards, calendars, posters, magazine covers, book covers, ceramic tiles, T-shirts, and as needlepoint and silkscreen designs. Storytellers are also used in countless ads for Indian art shops and galleries. Cordero has reacted to the manufacturing of the storyteller image: "They call them Storytellers, but they don't even know what it means. They don't even know it's my grandfather."

Like it or not, Cordero's storyteller dolls have made her famous and brought people from all over the world to her adobe home in Cochiti Pueblo where she makes and sells her dolls. She has said: "I am so proud and pleased and thankful about my 'Little People'; they have brought so many people to my house."

PABLITA VELARDE

◆ ◆ ◆

Santa Clara Painter
(1918 – 70)

I'm always preaching "Get your education." In the last few years there's been a lot of painters coming up. Somewhere along the line I imagine they decided, "If that old lady can do it, I can too ."

—Pablita Velarde,
from "Someday It Will All Be a Dream" (1989)

Pablita Velarde was born on September 19, 1918 in Santa Clara Pueblo, New Mexico, a centuries-old village, or pueblo, on the west bank of what is now called the Rio Grande. She was the third daughter born to Herman, a farmer and trapper, and Marianita Velarde. Four days after Pablita was born, Qualupita, her father's mother who was a medicine woman, performed a traditional naming ceremony and named her Tse Tsan, or "Golden Dawn" in English. When Tse Tsan was only three years old, her mother died from tuberculosis, an infection of the lungs. Pueblo people knew how to cure many kinds of sicknesses, but not this killing disease. In 1921, medicines, Native or non-Indian, were not yet available to cure this disease.

Not long after her mother died, Tse Tsan suffered an illness that took away her eyesight for nearly two years. She regained her eyesight, although her left eye was permanently weak. She also gained a passion for looking at everything. Despite the weakness in her eye, Tse Tsan became a sharp observer of her Santa Clara Pueblo, especially the sacred dances that took place in the village plaza. She watched traditional corn, animal, and eagle dances. She watched the slow procession of masked kachina dancers along a fixed course. She knew the men impersonated kachinas, spirits central to Pueblo and Hopi religions who are responsible for rain, the growth of corn and other crops, and the continuity of life. She watched every dance movement and dance circuit pattern. She looked at sacred body painting in traditional designs. She observed the kilts worn by men in ceremonies, woven of cotton and embroidered with colored yarn. She looked at the black dresses, called mantas, worn by the women in ceremonies, their tablitas, thin headboards of wood, woven belts and white buckskin boots. She gazed at evergreen branches, drums, rattles, and other sacred ritual objects. She watched and learned about the symbols for the four directions (north, south, east, west), each of which is designated by a color, animal, bird, mountain, and natural occurrence. She watched and learned the symbols for corn, seeds, clouds, sacred mountains, lightning, sun, moon, stars, animals, and birds. Without realizing it, Tse Tsan had "photographed" into her mind all the details of the dances she saw in the village plaza. Later, these childhood picture-memories played an important part in her paintings.

When Tse Tsan was about six, her father, unable to care for his daughters while he farmed and trapped, boarded them for the school year at St. Catherine's Indian School in Santa Fe, 30 miles south of Santa Clara. It was no surprise that Herman took his daughters there. In Santa Clara, Tse Tsan and her family attended ancient Pueblo dances and attended Catholic mass at the old mission church of adobe. On St. Clare's day, August 12, the family took part in a mass and Pueblo dances. Tse Tsan explained:

> Indians ignore one religion and then go into another. They'll ignore the Christian and pay attention to the Indian, then they'll come back to the Christian and ignore the Indian. It's like being in a house with two different rooms. They're different rooms, but they're the same house.

In kindergarten, the nuns soon renamed Tse Tsan *Pablita*, the Spanish word for "Pauline," the female name for "Paul," a Christian saint. She had to learn English because the nuns did not speak Tewa, her own language. It took several days for six-year-old Tse Tsan to get used to her new identity as Pablita and several weeks to get used to the "linguistic gibberish" (English) surrounding her.

Herman visited his children only twice during the first year of school, but he brought them home during the summers. Since Herman had no sons, Pablita and her sisters learned how to help him farm his fields. By horseback, the girls hauled water for drinking and cooking from Santa Clara Creek up to the flat mountain top where their father was raising corn, squash, and beans. They led cattle in and out of their pens. Pablita and her sisters did find time to play in the ancient cliff dwellings, which included at one time a house with 2,000 rooms. Running among the abandoned caves, the girls saw petroglyphs, ancient drawings scratched on the rocks. Again, Pablita stored their designs away in her mind.

Pablita and her sisters worked and played during the day, but on summer nights, their father, a respected storyteller entertained them with traditional stories. He told them about the creation of Santa Clara Pueblo people on earth and about the creation of the sun, moon, stars, plants, animals, and much, much more. Because she heard her father's stories more than once, Pablita learned the traditional beliefs of her people. She stored in her mind Herman's stories about the ancient ones.

While she was home during the summer, Pablita also spent time with her grandmother in the pueblo learning many traditions and skills from the woman who had named her when she was four days old. She watched the older woman roast gypsum rock in an outdoor oven, crush it into a powder, and make it into whitewash. Pablita's relatives used the mixture to paint the walls of the houses. They decorated the inside walls with colorful pigments from clay. Pablita watched her aunts make the distinctive black, shiny pottery for which Santa Clara is known and then tried it herself.

When summer ended, Pablita returned to school. In 1932, at 13, she left St. Catherine's and moved across town to a school run by the Bureau of Indian Affairs. There, she learned about the world of art from Dorothy Dunn, a teacher of Indian arts (see chapter on Oscar Howe for more information on Dunn). Dunn taught them about colors, design, paint brushes, drawing, and grinding raw clays and stones to make their own pigments. She encouraged the youngsters to draw outlines with pencil or charcoal and fill them in with opaque watercolor (tempera). Dunn encouraged students to draw figures from memories of reservation life, not from models, and to use their own tribal symbols. And she discouraged them from learning about the way non-Indians did art. Pablita, who spent her childhood memorizing everything she saw, had no problem responding to Dunn's teachings. Beginning in 8th grade and continuing up to the present, she searched her memory and found scenes of pueblo life that made their way onto paper and canvas. Her early drawings recreated the daily work of Santa Clara women. Soon Pueblo ceremonials became a favorite subject.

At the end of 8th grade, some of Pablita's paintings were exhibited in an all-Indian art show at the Museum of New Mexico. Olive Rush, an artist, liked Pablita's work and invited her and two other students to paint murals on masonite panels for an important exhibit taking place in Chicago in 1933 called the "Century of Progress." Many people saw Pablita's oil painting of a Santa Clara girl. After only one year of classes, Pablita had more requests to do art projects. And she became a better and better artist because she studied, sketched, and planned her work and learned how to use more art materials.

While Pablita attended the Santa Fe Indian School, she was the only girl who took all of the art classes in Dorothy Dunn's studio. She made her older sister Rosita enroll in Dunn's art classes with her so she

> wouldn't be the only girl in there. The boys at class used to be so mean about it, and would say, "Go get a job in the kitchen," stuff like that . . . Rosita got married after a few months but [Pablita] stayed on . . . The second year there were a few more girls that got brave enough and joined so it was better.

Traditional Pueblo people viewed painting as a male activity. Women made clay pots, but the men decorated them and only men painted sacred murals on the kiva (sacred chamber) walls. According to one biographer who has written about Pablita, "By working as an artist, Pablita was behaving in a way that was different from other Pueblo girls. She was considered a rebel, someone who does not act like everyone else." She was interested in graduating from the Santa Fe Indian School, but her father, who feared Pablita would not earn money because all she did was paint, had her transfer to Espanola High School. It offered business classes and the Sante Fe Indian School did not.

Pablita moved home while she went to Espanola, but she found it hard to adjust after living in boarding schools for more than 10 years. After taking all the business courses the high school offered, she transferred back to Santa Fe Indian School, graduating in 1936, the first in her family to get a high school diploma. After working for two years at Santa Clara as an assistant day-school instructor and then as a nanny for Ernest Thompson Seton, a founder of the Boy Scouts in the United States, she received two commissions. One was to help paint a mural for Maisel's jewelry store in Albuquerque.

The second commission came about when Dale Stuart King asked her to paint murals for the U.S. Park Service at Bandelier National Monument, a short distance from her pueblo. By remembering the stories she heard as a child, she created paintings that rank as ethnological studies so filled are they with extraordinary details about Pueblo daily life, seasonal activities and ceremonies, religious and political organization, and craft making. Velarde worked a wealth of Native lore into her paintings. She portrayed drum making, smithing, tanning, dyeing buckskin, beadwork, basket making, and drilling and stringing turquoise beads. She showed cultivated and wild plants with ritual significance and use; she depicted the plants used for craft purposes. She showed the inner workings of Pueblo religious life by painting a ceremonial rabbit hunt and a kiva filled with men. She painted summer and winter ceremonial dances carefully showing the regalia, sacred objects, and other symbols associated with them. She left nothing out. Whatever the ceremonial dance group, she gave them the proper clothing from hairdo to moccasins.

In 1940 the Park Service let Velarde go because of budget cuts, and she returned to Santa Clara. While living in her home, which she paid for with her own money and built with family help, she made some money selling paintings and decorating drums. Because she wanted a better job, she went to Albuquerque and worked as a switchboard operator for the Bureau of Indian Affairs office. There she met Herbert Hardin, an Anglo security guard, and the two were married on St. Valentine's Day, 1941.

By 1946, Velarde, with two children (one of whom, Helen Hardin, became a renowned artist herself) returned to Santa Clara from California, where her husband was studying criminology, because she was bothered by asthma. Because the family needed money to cover expenses in California and New Mexico, Velarde got her old job back at Bandelier. After long hours of study, she painted more ethnological scenes for the Park Service. Finally in 1947, Herbert joined the Albuquerque police force and the family was reunited and settled into a small house.

During the 1950s, sitting at her kitchen table in Albuquerque, Velarde perfected her "earth paintings." After collecting rocks and clays from all over New Mexico, she pounded them into powders, mixed them with white glue and water, and painted as many as seven layers of the granular mix on pieces of masonite. After outlining the forms in the painting, she added a surface coat to preserve the finish of the painting, and then framed each work herself. Earth paintings might show an isolated figure against undefined space or they might be totally abstract, composed of intricate symbols.

Velarde's paintings, done in either tempera or earth pigments, are famous for reporting details. Once, she explained that her paintings were "documentary, I guess. I think if I leave enough paintings it will be an education for everybody about very true things that happened in the pueblo."

Because Velarde was a celebrity, with newspapers reporting details about her career, she received many invitations to make personal appearances, some on television. She joined an

Pablita Velarde of Santa Clara Pueblo standing beside one of her earth paintings. (Photograph courtesy of the Museum of New Mexico, negative number 16927.)

organization that helped women improve their ability to give public speeches. At first Herbert enjoyed the public recognition Pablita received for her work, but he became resentful of the attention and the time she spent making her paintings and giving her speeches. During an unhappy period in her marriage, which ended in divorce in 1959, Pablita returned to the pueblo. Here she sought out her father and encouraged him to retell his stories, which she wrote down in English and illustrated in a book. One of the first illustrations she did for the book took the grand prize at the Gallup Inter-Tribal Indian Ceremonial in 1955. Her friend Dale Stuart King, who hired her for the Bandelier jobs, liked her book of stories and published them in 1960 as *Old Father, the Story Teller*. The book was also chosen as one of the best Western books of 1960.

Over the years Pablita Velarde has won many prizes for her work. In 1948, she won her first important award at the Philbrook Art Center in Tulsa, Oklahoma. In 1954 the French government awarded her the Palmes Académiques for her outstanding contributions to art along with Maria Martinez, the first time a foreign government had recognized Indian art. The next year, she took the grand prize and three first prizes at the Inter-Tribal Indian Ceremonial in Gallup. She took a Grand Award at the Scottsdale, Arizona, national annual exhibition in 1965. In 1968, the Philbrook gave her its coveted Waite Phillips Trophy that recognized her career achievements. In 1977, Velarde received the New Mexico Governor's Award for Outstanding Achievement in the Visual Arts. And in 1990, the Philadelphia-based Women's Caucus for Art gave her its annual award, the first Native American artist so recognized.

Velarde is still grinding stones into powders for her earth paintings and may yet win even more honors for her paintings that truly educate people about Pueblo culture.

BILL REID

◆ ◆ ◆

Haida Carver and Goldsmith
(1920 –$\mathcal{86}$)

*When I work, I am trying my best to get inside a traditional
artist's skin, an old-time artist, and do what he would have
done with the benefit of modern technology.*
　　　　　　　—Bill Reid, from *Bill Reid* (1986)

Bill Reid was born on January 12, 1920, in Victoria, British Columbia, to Sophia Gladstone, a Haida woman, and William Ronald
Reid. William Reid had been born in Michigan to German and
Scottish parents and had later become a naturalized Canadian. He
left home at 16 and began an itinerant career that eventually took
him to northern British Columbia. At 40, he met Bill's mother who
was then a schoolteacher. Gladstone was Haida, a people who
inhabited the Queen Charlotte Islands and the southern part of
Prince of Wales Island, Alaska. The Haida were one of a number
of Indian nations living in villages of large houses and totem poles
facing the sea that stretched along the Northwest coastline from
British Columbia northward to Alaska. This land was rich in food.
"Even today, only a stupid man could starve on this coast, and
today is not as it was," Bill Reid once wrote about the Northwest
coast. The land was rich in timber, especially cedar, that Native
master carvers and apprentices turned into houses, boats, boxes,
and cooking pots. "You can build from the cedar tree the exterior
trappings of one of the world's great cultures. Above all, you can

build totem poles, and the people of the northwest coast built them in profusion . . . " wrote Reid, who eventually did the same.

None of her people's traditions impressed English-speaking Sophia Gladstone, educated in a Canadian Methodist residential school; she took little pride in being Haida. According to Bill Reid, his mother:

> learned the major lesson taught the native peoples of our hemisphere during the first half of this century, that it was somehow sinful and debased to be, in white terms, an Indian, and [she] certainly saw no reason to pass any pride in that part of their heritage on to her children.

Bill, dressed in sailor suits and gloves by his mother, was a major disappointment to his rough-and-tough father. Bill, in turn, disliked his father. In 1933, Bill's mother left her husband and Bill never saw his father again. About this time, like his mother, who supported her three children by setting up a business designing clothes for fashionable families in Victoria, he started making things with his hands.

Bill's education was entirely in the European–North American society of his father. After he attended kindergarten in Victoria, the family moved, owing to his father's work; Bill went to elementary school in Hyder, Alaska, a frontier mining town. He wound up attending high school back in Victoria, graduating in 1934, and studying in a general arts program at Victoria College until 1937. None of the Canadian schools Reid attended gave him an education in his Haida identity. When Bill was 23, despite his mother's lack of interest in her Haida heritage, he set off for Haida Gwaii ("Haida land," the Haida Indians' name for the Queen Charlotte Islands) on the first of a lifelong series of trips to educate himself about his Native side.

In Skidegate, a Haida village on the Queen Charlotte Islands, he met Charles Gladstone, his grandfather, a silversmith who had learned his craft from elders such as Charlie Edenshaw (1839–1920), the renowned carver, who had taken him in as a youth. Through his mother, Reid was Edenshaw's great nephew. Reid saw and handled Edenshaw's tools, some fitted with handles of bone or ivory, that his grandfather had inherited. Reid developed a bond with his grandfather, one he never experienced with his father, even though the two could barely communicate. Gladstone spoke Haida and Reid English. Through his friendship with his grandfather, Reid met older Haida men and women who remembered their traditions. He began to identify with the Haida people, despite his mother's displeasure.

Reid had left home when he was 20, and because of his command of the English language and his speaking voice, he became a radio broadcaster, a career that lasted 16 years. In 1948, while working for the Canadian Broadcasting Corporation (CBC) in Toronto, he was attracted to courses offered at Ryerson Institute of Technology, located near his office. Since he worked at night, Reid could enroll in day classes. For two years he studied the techniques of European jewelry making. While he was in Toronto, he frequented the Royal Ontario Museum to visit a totem pole standing in a stairwell. The totem pole was from Tanu, his grandmother's village. Reid wrote that that village, now vanished, "may have been the crowning gem of west coast material culture." For Reid, "things began to come together in that pole."

In 1951, Bill and his first wife went back to Vancouver where he worked for CBC until 1958, chiefly in radio announcing. On one occasion, he aired the eulogy for his grandfather who died in 1954. At his grandfather's funeral in Skidegate, he finally had his first encounter with the work of Charles Edenshaw. He visited his great aunt who had two gold bracelets made by the famed carver. Reid's life was never the same after he saw them.

Soon after his grandfather's funeral, Reid joined the British Columbia Provincial Museum team that went north to save totem poles from abandoned village sites on the Queen Charlotte Islands. In 1955, he went to Tanu and Skedans, and in 1957 to St. Anthony Island. Invited by anthropologist Wilson Duff to spend two weeks at the museum carving a copy of a Haida pole, Reid worked on it for 10 days with Mungo Martin (1881–1962), an experienced totem pole carver from Fort Rupert. Directed by Martin, a Kwakiutl Indian (a tribe also living around the Queen Charlotte Islands with traditions similar to the Haida), to "carve there," Bill Reid took naturally to monumental wood carving. Reid especially valued the association with a carver who had grown up within his tribal tradition and who was determined to keep the old ways from being forgotten.

After leaving the CBC in 1958, Reid devoted himself full time to producing Haida art. First, he started with a large-scale public undertaking. He spent three and a half years as designer and director of a project to recreate a section of a Haida village with totem poles on the University of British Columbia campus. In a carving shed, Reid and his assistants produced monumental house and mortuary poles. Bill Reid had the remarkable ability to teach himself the art of Haida totem pole design and carving.

After he completed carving massive totem poles, Reid scaled down and started his own jewelry business in Vancouver, making intricate gold, platinum, and diamond bracelets, earrings, brooches, rings, and boxes. Again, Reid had to teach himself, this time about Haida design traditions. By the 1950s, there were no longer any Haida alive who fully understood Haida design principles. Their population had sharply declined by the late 1800s because of disease, and their culture had been broken down by harsh Canadian laws. Reid studied objects in museums and read ethnographies written by non-Indian anthropologists to find out about his people's design traditions. Spending hours pouring over photographs and illustrations in old ethnography books, Reid's earliest brooches copied tattoos—a common practice among Haida—that he found reproduced in a 1905 book about Haida ethnography. He spent hours looking at exceptional pieces in cases of the old British Columbia Provincial Museum and translated what he saw into brooches. Reid admitted that he "built up an unrepayable debt to the late Edenshaw, whose creations [he] studied, and in many cases, shamelessly copied, and through those works [he] began to learn something of the underlying dynamics of Haida art . . . " Slowly, Reid reconstructed the formal and complex principles of Haida designs and reversed the demise of a great cultural tradition. His method—copying the old masters' works—was the traditional way of learning among Northwest Coast people.

The earliest jewelry made on the Northwest Coast was mostly bracelets made by melting down coins, pouring the liquid silver into molds, and hammering the resulting mass of metal into strips that were then shaped into bracelets using wooden benders. Finally, the bracelets were engraved and carved with family crest designs. Reid followed nearly the same procedure except he used manufactured sheets of gold and silver, an engraver's block, and modern engraving tools. And he invented his own "bracelet bender." After a fellowship year in London that improved his goldsmithing techniques, he returned to Canada and made brooches and pendants, cuff links, earrings, and many, many bracelets, the kind of jewelry commonly worn by Haida women of high rank. But he extended the Haida tradition of two-dimensional bracelets and transformed them into small, three-dimensional wearable sculptures. In true Haida style, the head of a creature dominates the bracelet. Reid pushed the face forward, raising it from a two-dimensional to a sculptural form. But always Reid "followed the rules" of form and composition developed over centuries by his Haida ancestors.

Making jewelry offered Reid a way to hold on to his tradition while earning a living within a consumer society. He also made boxes in silver or gold inspired by traditional chests, boxes, and bowls that were displayed in villages during great feasts and winter ceremonies. Indeed, Reid's study of Haida art allowed him to become a part of the community that his mother left behind. In Reid's words, he tried to achieve that "sudden aching sense of identity with the distant cousin who first lovingly made . . . the elegant line, the subtle curve, the sure precise brush stroke."

Reid liked to do things well and attached great importance to technical perfection and workmanship. "Well-making," as he referred to it, was a central quality he recognized in the work of his ancestors. He also was fascinated with the tools required for his art. His ancestors made their own tools with their hands and ingenuity. He, too, made or adapted existing tools for engraving or for making hinges and clasps on jewelry pieces. Like his great-uncle Charles Edenshaw, he added hand- carved handles to his tools.

By 1977, Reid wanted to repay a debt to his ancestors and show his gratitude for the successes that derived from his Haida traditions. He carved a totem pole for his mother's village of Skidegate, the first to be erected there in 100 years. In June of 1978, the 55-foot pole was raised in front of the new Band Council Administration building; the pole looked out to sea in the same location as his grandfather's one-room workshop. It took Reid, now hampered by Parkinson's disease that was diagnosed in 1973, nine months of work, spread over two years, to complete. He carved figures drawn from Haida ancient stories: Grizzly Bear and Bear Mother with their cubs, Raven, Frog, Killer Whales, and Dogfish (shark), one of the crests of Reid's grandfather. Reid often carved these creatures, which also appeared in Edenshaw's carvings as well as his grandfather's. Raven was an especially personal symbol to Reid as it was the clan (social division) to which his grandmother belonged and had been celebrated by Edenshaw in many of his carvings. The community arranged a celebration for the pole-raising day, feeding 1,500 guests dinner.

Although Reid considers himself to be primarily a goldsmith, he has created massive and miniature works in wood, ivory, argillite (a kind of stone), and bronze. He did large outdoor commissions in the early 1980s. *Killer Whale,* a bronze inhabiting its own pool outside the Vancouver Aquarium in Stanley Park and *Mythic Messengers,* a bronze work commissioned by Teleglobe Canada for its building in Burnaby, British Columbia, required new technical procedures of Reid. He prepared scale models, made sectional molds, and had them cast at a foundry. The plaster form of the killer whale in the Vancouver Aquarium went to a foundry in New York where it took seven months to cast, finish, and give it a patina (a greenish film like that which develops on old copper and bronze).

In 1986, Reid carved a massive, 50-foot-long war canoe, a major undertaking of time, energy, and money. The canoe, on display at the World Exposition in Vancouver, again reflected his sense of identity with his forebears who rode down Queen Charlotte Sound in their huge canoes. Another canoe, a bronze boat some 20 feet in length, filled with people and eight mythological creatures was installed in the courtyard of the Canadian Embassy on Pennsylvania Avenue in Washington, D.C.

Bill Reid and his sculpture The Raven and the First Men *in 1980.* (Photograph courtesy of the University of British Columbia, Museum of Anthropology)

Reid works with younger artists who learn directly from him by assisting him as apprentices. Others watch him work, repeating the time-honored way Native cultures passed on their traditions.

Reid, whose art ranges from miniature brooches to four-and-a-half-ton carved wooden sculptures, also retold his own version of ancient stories about Haida mythological creatures and illustrated them with pencil drawings. Reid's pencil drawings for the book *The Raven Steals the Light* (1984) were like his carvings, intricate, dense, the space filled up with interlocking forms.

Even though Reid spent most of his life on the edge of Haida society, he has been an ardent spokesman for the Haida people. He supports Haida land claims and has campaigned actively for the preservation of South Moresby Island, part of Haida ancestral lands. During 1987, he stopped work on the bronze canoe for the Canadian Embassy to protest a dispute between Canada and the provincial government of British Columbia over logging in the southern half of the Queen Charlotte Islands. Both sides had ignored the claims of the Haida people.

Reid, acclaimed as one of the greatest living Native artists and a symbol of the Northwest Coast art revival, ranks among Canada's most important sculptors, white or Indian. For his success in reviving and bringing recognition to ancient Northwest Coast art forms and for his creativity and innovations, he has won countless awards. Five Canadian universities have conferred honorary doctorates. On his 65th birthday, the mayor of Vancouver declared Bill Reid Day.

CHARLES LOLOMA

♦ ♦ ♦

Hopi Jeweler
(1921–1991)

*I feel a strong kinship to stones, not just the precious and
semi-precious stones I use in my jewelry, but the humble
stones picked up at random while on a hike through the hills
or a walk along the beach. I feel the stone and think, not to
conquer it, but to help it express itself.*
—Charles Loloma, from "Charles Loloma" (1975)

Charles Loloma was born on January 7, 1921 in the village of
Hotevilla on the Third Mesa of the Hopi Reservation, or Land of
the Peaceful People, in northeastern Arizona at the southern end
of Black Mesa. There, two other steep, flat-topped mesas (First
Mesa and Second Mesa) rise sharply above the desert floor and
dry valleys. Scattered across the three mesas are Hotevilla, considered a tenacious village in terms of the people holding on to and
preserving ancient Hopi customs, and the other villages—the
homeland of Hopi for centuries. Like his ancestors, Loloma grew
up in one of the small brown houses made of stone that seemed to
grow out of the mesa rock formation. His parents were Rex of the
Sand and Tobacco Clan and Rachel of the Badger Clan. Like his
mother, Charles belonged to the Badger Clan. Hopi clans, named
for animals, birds, or other parts of nature, are groups of people
united through the female line. Loloma's father made moccasins
and was an accomplished weaver. His mother was an accom-

plished basket maker. Charles's grandfather Loloma (which means "many beautiful colors" in the Hopi language), had gone with four other Hopi chiefs to Washington, D.C. in June of 1890 to try to get the Indian commissioner to protect those mesas with their villages of stone and the rights of Hopi people.

Loloma grew up Hotevilla, a traditional Hopi village where people centered their life around the raising of corn and worshiping in ancient ceremonies that take place year round. Loloma's family believed that if people did not perform certain ceremonies at prescribed times in prescribed ways, rain would not fall, corn would not grow, animals and human beings would not be fertile. By faithfully participating in the ritual cycle with prayers and offerings, Charles's family knew the spirits would reciprocate with rain so the crops would grow. Like other Hopi boys raised in a traditional way, Loloma was initiated into a Kachina society, which begins the religious life of all Hopi girls and boys and introduces the children to a new status in the tribe. He fully participated in the ceremonial life of his village and was a member of the Snake Society, a religious society that performed, every two years in August, an ancient sacred 16-day dance, a petition to rain spirits to send moisture.

Growing up at Hotevilla, Loloma felt a great kinship with nature, even for "humble pebbles picked up at random while on a hike through the hills." Eventually these "humble stones" made their way into his creations. And so, too, did the colors, textures, and shapes of the earth of Third Mesa.

Charles Loloma's parents wanted their son educated in both the Hopi and non-Indian traditions, so he attended day school in the village. Here teachers recognized his artistic talent and encouraged him to draw and paint. While he was at Hopi High School in Oraibi, Arizona, he studied art with the Hopi artist Fred Kabotie, one of the masters of traditional Native American painting. Kabotie encouraged Loloma. After transferring to the Phoenix Indian School in Arizona, where he graduated in 1940, he studied with Lloyd Kiva New, a noted Indian craftsman. At summer school in Fort Sill, Oklahoma, he studied with Olle Nordmark, a noted muralist.

In 1939, when he was 18 years old and still in high school, he worked with Kabotie and Rene d'Harnoncourt from the Museum of Modern Art in New York City, painting murals for the Federal Building in the 1939 Golden Gate Exposition in San Francisco. The next year, he assisted Kabotie in painting reproductions of murals discovered on the walls of kivas (sacred ceremonial rooms) in ancient Hopi Pueblo ruins at Awatovi in northeastern Arizona. (These murals are now displayed at the Denver Art Museum.) That same year, he illustrated the book *Hopihoya* by Edward Kennard.

In 1941, Loloma, like others, was drafted. He served in the U.S. Army until 1945, spending three years as an engineer in the Aleutian Islands. After his discharge, he and his wife, Otellie (a ceramicist whom he had married in 1942), returned to her Hopi village of Shipaulovi on Second Mesa. In 1945, with monies from the GI Bill, Charles and Otellie attended the School for American Craftsmen at Alfred University in Alfred, New York. Charles studied design, mechanical drawing, marketing, and ceramic chemistry. Since women usually make pottery in Hopi culture, Loloma broke from tradition. While he was at Alfred, Charles experimented with shale clays and turned them into glazes when he fired them at high temperatures. After Alfred, he completed a two- year Whitney Foundation Fellowship, which gave him time to study the clays of the Hopi area. For several years, 1954–60, he and his wife ran a successful pottery shop in Scottsdale, Arizona, while Charles also taught part time at Arizona State University, the University of Arizona, and summer courses in Sedona, Arizona. Classroom teaching and running the shop gave Loloma experience in selling and talking with people. But even while he was making and selling pottery, Loloma really wanted to make jewelry.

When he was a boy, Charles had watched his grandfather pour molten silver into sandstone molds to create buckles, bracelets, and conchas (belts made of silver disks strung onto leather). Loloma saw beauty in the textures of the sandstone molds, and when he began making pieces of jewelry, he incorporated textures into his overall designs. Loloma began making his first pieces during the early 1950s, while he was a potter. He taught himself traditional silversmithing with the help of John Adair's book, *The Navajo and Pueblo Silversmiths*. He started out using silver because it cost less than gold. At first, he made pieces that used Hopi silver overlay techniques and designs from Hopi pottery. But that didn't last for long. He started casting silver pieces from molds carved from tufa stone, a porous limestone that has an imperfect surface. Rather than filing and buffing the silver to a smooth and shining surface, as was the custom, he let the natural grain of the tufa stone with its imperfections remain imprinted on the silver. (Loloma also used the lost wax method, sculpting a piece in wax, encasing it in casting plaster, burning the wax out, and pouring molten silver into the mold. The mold is automatically destroyed in this process because it has to be broken to get the cast silver piece out.

When Loloma could afford to buy some gold, he set stones, even potsherds, in gold bezels "to warm them up." Unlike other jewelers, Loloma saw no problem mixing gold, a non-traditional metal, with silver and made pieces using both metals. After he could afford it, he set stones completely in gold. Loloma broke other barriers of tradition. He built bracelets and rings with "height" from materials such as coral from Italy, lapis lazuli from Afghanistan, elephant tusk ivory from Africa, turquoise from the Southwest, or stones, shell, bone, and ironwood he picked up while walking through the Arizona desert—a design that emerged gradually over 15 years of experimenting. He combined many contrasting colors of stone of varied shapes, some small chunks, others long and slim, all cut to fit the curvature of a bracelet or ring. Sometimes, he lined up the pieces and rounded them to the same height so they had a striped effect. Other times, he stacked the uneven slabs next to one another so they resembled a jagged landscape. But always, according to Susan Fair who wrote an article about Loloma for the premiere issue of *American Indian Art*, "The pieces are channeled together not unlike an interlocking jig-saw puzzle, and secured by a clean Loloma bezel . . . one of the most complex creations on the contemporary Indian jewelry market today."

Loloma also hid stones on the inside of his creations. A bracelet might have a mosaic of inlaid turquoise and coral on the inside "a secret only the wearer knows." Or Loloma might conceal a diamond inside a chunk of fossilized ivory. He hid these stones because he believed people, like his work, had hidden beauty inside them. His second wife, Georgia, explained the hidden stones:

> Charles called these "inner gems" and they represent the collective personal beauty, the value system, the choices that we make as individuals about who we become, that is your inner beauty, it's your inner gems.

During the 1950s and 1960s, Loloma broke down barriers that kept Indian artists and art locked up in rules as to what they should create. Like Oscar Howe, whose rule-breaking painting was rejected in 1958 by an important annual exhibition for "not being Indian," Loloma's jewelry was rejected at first as well. The Gallup (New Mexico) Inter-tribal Ceremonial Exhibition felt the materials he used were not "Indian" and neither were his designs. Loloma ignored the rules and successfully challenged and changed the definitions of what was considered Indian art. By the 1960s, his jewelry pieces were accepted in exhibitions, and he had, according to art educator Winona Garmhausen, a national reputation for "almost unsurpassable talent in design and technique in the field of various metals and ceramics" and was considered "exceptional in approaching problems of design through Indian traditions, while at the same time innovating departures for contemporary use."

Loloma paved the way for other Indian metalsmiths to express their cultures in new ways. Not only jewelers have been inspired by Loloma and his free-spirited designs. By challenging the definitions of what was considered "Indian" art, he won acceptance for Indian artists as well. After George Boyce, superintendent of the newly created Institute of American Indian Arts (opened in 1962 on the site of the old Studio of the Santa Fe Indian School), hired Loloma to head the department of plastic arts and the sales department (where student art was sold), Loloma inspired young artists in another way. He noticed that his talented students had difficulty opening up and talking to people because Indians had learned "through anthropology that all Indians are supposed to be introverts . . . " He led a speech class in which students taped and listened to their voices.

Loloma, who participated in ancient Hopi ceremonies in the high desert country, had a zest for the finest life had to offer, from driving a yellow Jaguar to dining in the world's finest restaurants to jetting all over Europe to see his jewelry modeled in fashion shows and displayed in solo exhibitions. Loloma, however, always returned to Hotevilla on Third Mesa. Indeed, in the midst of his successful 1971 Paris show, he flew home to take part in the Powamu (Bean Dance), a sacred ceremony lasting 16 days in February.

In 1966 Loloma began construction of a studio and gallery. It was here that he worked until 1986 when he was injured in a car accident, leaving him unable to work, and had to close his shop. Loloma died in June 1991. He lived, however, to see his work command recognition both in the United States and abroad. During the 1960s, he won first prize seven years in a row at the prestigious Scottsdale (Arizona) National Indian Arts Exhibition. His work was so exquisite that President Lyndon Johnson presented gifts of his jewelry to the queen of Denmark and the wife of President Marcos of the Philippines. In 1971, in addition to his second Paris show, Loloma had a one-man show at the Heard Museum in Phoenix, Arizona. In 1972, Loloma was featured in the NET film *Three Indians*. In 1974, he was the subject of the PBS film *Loloma*. He was appointed to the Arizona Commission on the Arts and Humanities in 1973. In late 1974, he spent five weeks as artist-in-residence in Japan. In 1990, he received the Arizona Governor's Award for his contributions to the arts in the state.

Note: The family of Charles Loloma prefers that no photograph accompany this chapter.

STANLEY R. HILL

◆ ◆ ◆

Mohawk Bone Carver
(1921–83)

*After doing a few carvings, the antlers and bones seem to come
alive. A whole new world opened to me. It appeared that any
discarded bone or antler could be transformed into a life-like
object of beauty.*

—Stanley Hill,
from "Bone Carvings by Stanley Hill" (1977–78)

Stanley R. Hill, a Mohawk of the Turtle Clan*, was born on
November 16, 1921 at Oshweken, near Brantford, Ontario, Canada, on the Six Nations Reservation. His mother Charlotte Hill had
a talent for making exceptional quilts and objects of cornhusk. His
father worked with wood while recuperating in England after
World War I. Stanley received his education at Oshweken until
1934, when, at the age of 13, he dropped out of school. Hill and his
father went to Buffalo, New York, to look for work as jobs were
scarce on the reservation. From the age of 13, Hill worked hard as
a laborer on truck and fruit farms in the Lewiston, New York, area
and then helped to build and paint houses for a man who later
became his father-in-law.

At 19, he became an apprentice ironworker in structural steel work
for the Bethlehem Steel Company, but World War II cut short the
apprenticeship. He joined the U.S. Navy after marrying Alma Wilson. The navy sent him to a metalsmith school in Boston where he

---

* A clan is a group of people descended from a common female or male ancestor.

studied "math, blueprints, machine shop techniques, and welding." He then went to San Francisco where he studied advanced welding and then deep sea diving. He graduated as a second class diver.

At the end of World War II, Hill, who did dangerous salvage diving in the South Pacific, left the navy with a first class in metals rating. Back in the United States, Hill became an ironworker, following in the footsteps of generations of Mohawk men before him, spending the next 33 years working in construction. Like these men, ironwork was more than just a way to make a living to Hill. In referring to themselves, Iroquois ironworkers (those of the Cayuga, Mohawk, Oneida, Onondaga, Seneca, and Tuscarora tribes) used the name in their own language, *Hodinoso:* ni, meaning "house builders."

Hill's Mohawk tribal ancestors built structures, called long-houses, some 200 feet in length in which people lived. They also built bridges so they could cross rivers both in Ontario, Canada and New York state, homeland of the Iroquois peoples. After log cabins were introduced in the 18th century, Seneca and other Hodinoso: ni adopted the technique and built some of the best cabins in New York. Ironworking has continued the construction tradition in the modern world, only now the lodges constructed are tall, not long, and the bridges longer and much higher above the water. The Mohawk people were the first of the Iroquois people to walk the iron, and it was bridgework that launched their career in construction. In 1850, the Grand Trunk Railway from Montreal to Kahnawake hired Mohawk men to work on the bridge. In 1886, Mohawk were again hired as laborers by the Dominion Bridge Company that constructed a bridge across the St. Lawrence River for the Canadian Pacific Railway. The company records reported that "They would walk a narrow beam high up in the air with nothing below them but the river which is rough there and ugly . . . and it wouldn't mean any more to them than walking on the solid ground."

Ironworking, however, or skywalking as it is called by the Mohawk and other Iroquois peoples who live in New York and Ontario, is a dangerous occupation full of great risk. "It brings out only the adventurous, the thrillseekers, who will face the danger, and have fun doing it. The Iroquois people have often been at the forefront to seek adventure." Death could be part of the job. Most ironworkers have fallen at least once from the steel and all know someone killed on the job. In 1907, 38 Mohawk fell 300 feet when the Quebec Bridge buckled and collapsed into the St. Lawrence River; 33 died. Ironwork provides an immediate opportunity to prove oneself, to show nerve and agility, to make the body work as hard as the mind, and to gain respect. Hill also has pointed out that "Indians are outdoor people not suited for factory work. Ironwork was more to their liking."

Hill's career as an ironworker really began in 1941 when, at the age of 20, his brother-in-law took him to get a work permit in Buffalo, New York. He first worked at the Huntly Power Station, but at the age of 23, because of his navy work, he qualified as a journeyman. Hill then became a foreman for the Buffalo Structural Steel Company and worked on most of the major buildings and bridges in the Buffalo area. He became a steel erection contractor and formed and became vice-president of his own company, Consolidated Steel Erectors of Tonawanda, New York. Many Iroquois men, including his own sons, worked for his company. The hard work, demanding, pressured, and competitive, led at times to hard drinking.

Hill learned fast that the skywalking was dangerous, and he knew full well that "If you fall, chances are you are going to get killed." He saved his brother-in-law from falling on their first job together. Years later, he saw his own son fall from the steel (luckily, his son survived). "Anyone can get hurt. The more you know, the less chance you have of getting hurt, but you have to spot danger before it happens."

Hill saw ironworking as a rite of passage, a challenge, a way to prove his manhood and gain respect, as had generations of Mohawk skywalkers before him, and as a way to provide for his family (he had a wife, four sons, and a daughter). He also felt that after he mastered ironworking, dealing with the Euroamerican world around him became easier. Ironwork gave Hill pride and self-confidence that enabled him to prove himself, not only to himself, but to others, especially to Euroamericans. Working iron provided Hill with a way to overcome the negative images people held about him and other Indians. He made enough money to "live like a white man," but he made it in a traditional Mohawk way. Hill has written "Ironwork was a way out, a way to become someone, to compete, to beat the white man . . . to compete with the society that we are stuck with." Ironworking also required hard work, a valued Indian tradition, and Hill had always believed in doing hard work and doing it well. He prided himself on his craftmanship, a trait that he later translated into his bone carvings.

Hill began his first attempts at carving while he worked in steel, carving animal heads on stainless steel rings. He entered a ring in an annual national Indian exhibition in Scottsdale, Arizona, and it won him fourth place. The sudden and tragic death of his second oldest son in a car accident made Hill take stock of his life. After more than three decades as a steelworker, he decided to leave that world, spend more time hunting, and support his family by carving. He worked mostly with deer antler and on occasion with moose and elk antlers. Sometimes he carved pieces from steer or whale vertebrae.

Hill became a full-time carver in 1974. He had no knowledge of the woodcarver's craft or the mask carving tradition of his own people before he took up carving because he had lived away from his reservation most of his life. Through trial and error, he taught himself how to carve using his own methods, trying different handmade tools until he discovered power drills whose fine bits enabled him to hollow out bone and antler.

Hill uses band saws to cut out rough shapes and Dremmel hobby tools to shape, drill, or buff pieces. He uses motorized wheel sanders and polishing rouge to create gleaming surfaces. He mounts his finished works on stone or hardwood bases.

Although Hill does not remember hearing traditional Mohawk stories as a child and does not spend time researching them, he carves traditional subject matter from Iroquois culture and history like the Tree of Peace (under which the Iroquois peoples buried their war hatchets and made peace among their nations), turtles (which figure in the Hodinoso:ni creation story), and Three Sisters (corn, bean, and squash spirits) who have sustained Iroquois people with food. Hill has said his ability to visualize these images

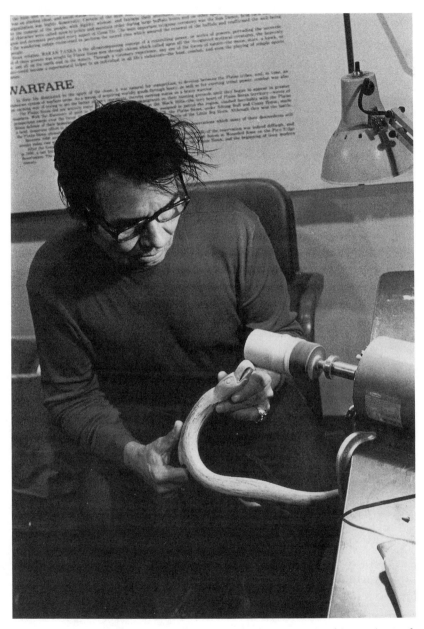

Stanley R. Hill, a Mohawk bone carver, shown demonstrating his carving style in 1977 at the Sioux Indian Museum in Rapid City, South Dakota. (Photograph courtesy of the U.S. Department of the Interior, Indian Arts and Crafts Board, Sioux Indian Museum and Crafts Center)

comes from knowledge bequeathed to him by his ancestors. Whatever the source of his imaginative carvings, he gives them great detail so they appear real. The eyes of the animals, remarkably life-like, amaze people. Early in his career, Hill realized the importance of the eyes in his animals and figures so he developed special stains for eyeballs from tea, coffee, tobacco, and waterproof ink.

Hill honors the spirits of the animals and plants he carves. When he was growing up, he grew corn and during the long years he worked as an ironworker, he planted gardens. Growing corn and other plants connected him to Iroquois tradition. He also has strong feelings for the animals he has observed and hunted for food. He feels plants and animals have a life force, or spirit, a belief that goes back to the Iroquois concept of *orenda*, the energy that the Iroquois believed to be part of all elements of nature—humans, plants, animals, and rocks.

While carving, Hill imagines that he is "extending the life of an animal" because he thinks of the antlers as being alive. In the sculpture *The Great Tree* carved out of moose antler in 1980, Hill depicted an eagle head on the surface of which is etched a tree with four roots representing the four cardinal directions—north, south, east, west—and symbolizing the fact that peace among the tribes had spread in all directions. By turning the antler into an eagle, Hill gave the antler a new life.

At first Hill created eagles with heads carved out of deer antler, and bodies suggested by the shape of the rack. Soon turtles, weasels, badgers, beavers, otters, squirrels, wolves, herons, deer, snipes, bear, buffalo, rams, and birds poured out of his imagination showing up on belt buckles, as handles for knives, as pendants, or on combs inspired by objects found in ancient Seneca sites. In the carving *The Three Sisters,* Hill gave the three agricultural spirits female faces entwined with vegetation that has elaborate details such as leaf veins, flower petals, kernels on the corn, beans in the pods, and squash on the vine. He has converted larger pieces of antler into turtles, one of the nine Iroquois clans and also Hill's personal clan. On the back of some of these turtles, he has carved each of the nine Iroquois clan animals. Hill also has carved works with historical basis such as *Descent of Sky Woman,* in which the traditional story of the creation of the Iroquois people is told, and *Burning of the Cornfields* based on actions taken in 1779 by U.S. Major General John Sullivan. Other works depict information from wampum belts that relate to ancient treaties. Hill also experiments with the finish on the surface of his pieces.

Hill wanted to do as well economically as he had in his iron-working days. He studied fairs, galleries, and exhibition shows and made inexpensive key chains for one market and major pieces worth thousands of dollars for other markets. Since he started carving bone and antler, Hill has created more than a thousand pieces. He works in a studio at his home in Grand Island, New York, and also has a shop on the Six Nations Reserve in Ontario, Canada. Two of his sons, Russell, who also left ironworking to do bone and antler carving, and Stan, Jr., carve and a family business has developed. Hill's daughter, Janet, has been his business manager. In addition, Hill's wife, Tam, has her own craft business and his son Richard paints, beads, and does featherwork.

Hill's works of art have been exhibited in galleries and museums throughout the United States and Canada. His work is represented in the Woodland Indian Cultural, Educational Center in Brantford, Ontario, the Indian Arts and Crafts Board in Washington, D.C., and in numerous private collections. In 1984, the Schoharie Museum of the Iroquois Indian mounted a retrospective of Hill's most important carvings. Hill, whose works have received international acclaim, has won more than 50 awards in major art shows in the United States and Canada. In 1975, only a year after he began carving full time, Hill received a First Place Award at the Northern Arts and Crafts Show in Buffalo, New York, and a First Place Award at the Seneca Fall Festival in Cattaragus, New York. In 1976, he received the Third Place Sculpture Award at the renowned Scottsdale, Arizona, 14th Annual Exhibition. In 1977, the Philbrook Art Center in Tulsa, Oklahoma, awarded him First Place in Sculpture at its prestigious 32nd annual artists' exhibition; the Phoenix-based Heard Museum twice—in 1979 and 1980—bestowed its First Place in Sculpture Award on Hill. More awards in sculpture have come from the art shows in Florida, Illinois, Oklahoma, South Dakota, and Toronto, Ontario.

EVA WOLFE

◆ ◆ ◆

Cherokee Rivercane Basket Weaver
(1922 – 5?)

I prefer rivercane as a basketweaving material because of the patterns I can see in the weaving.

—Eva Wolfe,
from "Doubleweave Rivercane Basketry by Eva Wolfe" (1978)

Eva Wolfe, a member of the Eastern band of Cherokee was born to Cherokee parents on July 24, 1922 in the Soco Community of the Qualla Indian Reservation in western North Carolina.

Before 1830, the Cherokee people, believed to be the largest tribe in the Southeast, lived in settlements in what is now Georgia, North Carolina, South Carolina, and Tennessee. During the Removal Period, when federal government policy forced Indians living east of the Mississippi River to move west of it, the Cherokee split into two bands. A large group, now called the Western Cherokee, settled in Indian Territory, now Oklahoma, and those 1,400 Cherokee who remained in the Southeast, Eva Wolfe's people, were gradually forced deeper into the Smoky Mountain area of North Carolina where they started life over again on small farms or in small settlements in the mountains.

Many lived in family groups in which at least one female member wove baskets for household and farm use. Some

Cherokee families traded their baskets for cloth, clothing, and food with Anglo-American farmers who lived on the borders of the Cherokee Nation. The farmers, who used the baskets in their homes and fields, sometimes resold them. Eventually, the basket trade became crucial to the economy of the Cherokee and resulted in social contacts between the non-Indian and Indian groups. Basket trading created opportunities for Cherokee and southern Appalachian people to sample one another's food and even try to speak one another's language.

The Eastern Band of Cherokee held on to the time-honored tradition of basket making, which they trace back to their creation stories. In these stories, baskets figure as essential tools for the first humans soon after the world was created. From ancient times to the end of the 19th century, when their lives were disrupted, Cherokee women, like Washo women, made baskets strictly to be used. Baskets figured in a person's life from birth to death. Written descriptions of Cherokee baskets appeared in the late 18th century when British traders such as James Adair in South Carolina sang the praises of "Cheerake" rivercane baskets. This quote is from 1775:

> They [Cherokee] make the handsomest clothes baskets I ever saw, considering their materials. They divided large swamp canes into long, thin narrow splinters, which they dye of several colours, and manage the workmanship so well, that both the inside and outside are covered with a beautiful variety of pleasing figures [now called doubleweave] . . . Formerly, those baskets which the Cheerake made, were . . . highly esteemed even in South Carolina, the politest of our colonies, for domestic usefulness, beauty, and skillful variety . . .

According to records from the late 1830s and early 1840s, the majority of Cherokee families owned from two to 20 baskets, most woven of split rivercane, that were used for carrying, winnowing, hulling, sifting, processing corn, and as sieves, bread trays, and storage containers for clothes. Rarely did these baskets have handles. Neither did the baskets traded to the Anglo farmers. Major changes in the late 19th and early 20th centuries soon altered Eastern Cherokee culture and the traditional baskets. The region's forests and rich mineral resources attracted investors eager to exploit them. Railroads brought vacationers on day excursions into the Smokies. In 1902, after the federal Indian office suggested that Cherokee be encouraged to produce crafts for cash, a tourist market for Cherokee baskets grew. Cherokee families who once traveled long distances to trade baskets with Anglo farmers for "potatoes, canned stuff, dried beans, apples, molasses, and once in a while, meat," stopped the practice. Instead, there was plenty of opportunity to sell baskets for cash to tourists. Since Anglo customers wanted handles, a European feature, Cherokee basket makers added wooden ones to "carrying baskets," an old style basket form, to please their customers. Within two years of the coming of the Southern Railroad in 1909, 40 Cherokee basket weavers reported cash income from part-time basketry sales.

Eva Wolfe was born by the time the annual Cherokee Indian fair drew large crowds of Cherokee and Anglo-Americans. When she was a girl, cash income from basket sales at the fair plus sales through such shops as the Southern Highlands Handicrafts Guild, founded in 1929, reached $10,000 a year total, providing a considerable income for some Qualla basket makers.

As a young girl, Eva first learned the art of basketry from her mother, who, like many Eastern Cherokee women of her time, was an accomplished weaver. She also learned from her aunt, Lottie Stamper, a notable Cherokee basket-weaving instructor who gave classes at the Cherokee Indian School, a government-run school serving Indian students from the Qualla Indian Reservation. After high school, Eva Wolfe also attended adult education classes on the reservation, where she first turned her attention to the doubleweave form of rivercane basketry.

One of the most difficult containers to make, a doubleweave basket requires the skillful weaving of one basket inside another, in one continuous weave of material. Although Cherokee basket makers were famous for their accomplishments in the art during the 1800s, the complex doubleweave had rapidly declined in production. During the 1940s, federal government agencies such as the Bureau of Indian Affairs and the Indian Arts and Crafts Board encouraged Cherokee people to revive doubleweave baskets. The federal agencies turned to members of the Qualla Arts and Crafts Mutual, Inc., urging them to learn the art before it was too late. Qualla was a Cherokee-owned tribal arts and crafts cooperative that had been organized in 1946 on the reservation. It provided basket weavers with a permanent place to sell their baskets and encouraged its artists to revive and improve the quality of traditional doubleweave baskets. During the late 1950s, when she realized there were only two older women who could make rivercane doubleweave containers, Wolfe learned the art "in order that it might be retained for future generations of Cherokee craftsworkers." Wolfe mastered the techniques of weaving one basket inside another as well as all other forms of rivercane basketry.

Making rivercane baskets takes an enormous amount of time even before a basket weaver sits down to pick up the first strip. It takes time for a basket weaver like Eva Wolfe to gather the raw materials from the woods and fields around her home. Sometimes the materials she needs require a long trip. Each April, Eva and her husband Amble went to Hayesville, North Carolina, 80 miles from their home to gather a truckload of cane from swampy areas. This would last Eva about three months. The people of Hayesville are glad to get rid of the rivercane.

It takes time for Wolfe to turn the cane into strips. Each stalk renders four strips for weaving once she "busts" it with a bush knife whose blade has been worn through years of use. Wolfe padded the handle well with black tape to prevent her hands from blistering. After scraping the strips with a pocket knife, Wolfe frequently dips them in water to keep them pliable.

It takes time for Wolfe to gather the plants whose roots provide dyes. April is a good time for Wolfe to gather a yearly supply of bloodroot, the plant native to the slopes around her home that supplies a reddish brown dye she uses in her basket designs. Whenever she needs it, Wolfe also extracts a dark brown dye from butternut tree roots in the vicinity of her home. In summer, she dyes her materials outside in a washtub. In the winter, she moves indoors and dyes them in a canner on a wood heater. All told, gathering, preparing, and dying the raw materials can account for half the time Wolfe needs to create a basket.

Once Wolfe has finished coloring the cane strips with bloodroot and butternut root dyes, she begins her weaving. Sometimes she spends the whole day weaving, sometimes only a half day, and sometimes not at all. Over the years, her 11 children have kept her busy as have other activities. Wolfe handles as many as 120 pieces of cane at a time, which she manipulates with a dexterity that amazes onlookers. She weaves darker and lighter pieces of cane into designs called Arrowhead, Bird's Eye, Chief's Daughter, and Cross on the Hill. The names Wolfe has assigned to her baskets sometimes vary from the design names other basket-weaving families use.

Wolfe's hard work in bringing doubleweave baskets to new heights of technical and aesthetic achievement has insured the survival of a difficult art form. Equally important to Eva Wolfe, selling baskets provided an income that made a better way of life possible for her, Amble, and their four daughters and seven sons. In her statement accompanying her exhibition of doubleweave rivercane baskets in December 1978, she wrote:

> In 1963, I was told that ten dollars was too high a price for one of my large singleweave cane waste baskets; now I sell one for a hundred dollars. At one time, the shops wouldn't buy my doubleweave baskets; now they are in great demand . . . I make more doubleweave baskets than anything else because they sell better.

Over the years, tourists and art collectors have bought Wolfe's rivercane shopping baskets, lidded storage containers, and knitting baskets with white oak swing handles. Cherokee people, too, favor her baskets and use them as purses, diaperbags, kitchen containers, special gifts, or offering plates in Cherokee churches. Today, the Qualla Arts and Crafts Mutual, Inc. (where baskets are by far the best-selling items) sells Wolfe's baskets (as well as the work of 100 other basket weavers) providing her with an income she can count on. As a member of the Qualla cooperative, now recognized as possibly the most

Eva Wolfe shown weaving a rivercane basket in 1969. (Photograph courtesy of the U.S. Department of the Interior, Indian Arts and Crafts Board)

outstanding Indian-owned-and-operated arts and crafts coop-erative in the United States, Wolfe earns money when her baskets are purchased. But she also earns extra benefits such as dividends and a percentage of the store's profits when surplus money is available to make the payments without hurting the operation of the business.

Mastering the doubleweave form of basketry has brought Eva Wolfe fame. In addition to numerous prizes won in competition at annual fairs held on the Qualla Indian Reservation, Wolfe was awarded in 1968 a first prize for a doubleweave basket exhibited at the U.S. Interior Department in Washington, D.C. In December of 1969, the Indian Arts and Crafts Board in cooperation with the Cherokee-reservation-based Qualla Arts and Crafts Mutual, Inc., organized the first one-person exhibition of her basketry. Nine years later, in 1978, the two organizations honored Wolfe again with a unique exhibition of only doubleweave containers. The second show resulted from the grant awarded her by the National Endowment for the Arts in 1977. In the exhibition brochure, Wolfe wrote:

> I lost interest in basket weaving during the illness and death of my father. But a grant from the National Endowment for the Arts in 1977 rekindled my desire to continue in the craft, which is a tradition of my people, and helped me secure materials for more baskets. I am proud that I was selected for this honor and have enjoyed making these doubleweave baskets for this special exhibition in appreciation for the grant.

In 1980, one of Wolfe's covered storage baskets of doubleweave rivercane was in the inaugural exhibition of some 300 traditional and contemporary objects by Appalachian artists at the Joe L. Evins Appalachian Center for Crafts in Cookeville, Tennessee. In 1989, Wolfe's home state of North Carolina recognized her outstanding contributions to basketry art by giving her a Folk Heritage Award. In October of 1993, she won the Grand Prize for a doubleweave basket at the Cherokee Fall Festival. True to her words, Eva Wolfe continues weaving baskets and ensures that her people's ancient tradition lives on.

JIMMY TODDY
(BEATIEN YAZZ)

◆ ◆ ◆

Navajo Painter
(c. 1928 or 1930 – ⁇)

*Even when I was small, I was sketching and chipping on the
canyon walls in the way of my old ancestors.*
—Beatien Yazz, from *Yazz: Navajo Painter* (1983)

Jimmy Toddy was born sometime between 1928 and 1930 near
Wide Ruins, Arizona, on the Navajo Reservation. His Navajo
father was known as Joe Toddy and, because his mother died
when he was very young, his grandmother raised him and his two
sisters. Jimmy grew up in hilly desert country filled with juniper
forests, cottonwood trees, canyons, sand, birds, and animals that
early on made their way into the little boy's paintings.

He also grew up near one of the largest Pueblo sites in the
Southwest built by the Anasazi who lived in Wide Ruins at the end
of the 13th century. These ancient people carved or painted their
drawings on the walls of canyons. Their petroglyphs, or rock
drawings, were everywhere to be found. When eight-year-old
Jimmy discovered their marks on stone while he was exploring the
washes and canyons, he imitated the ancients and scratched a
horse onto a rock. Sallie and Bill Lippincott, an Anglo couple who
owned the Wide Ruins trading post, watched the boy chipping on

the rock and made a gift of art supplies to him. As he filled the pad of paper with crayon or watercolor drawings, he experimented with colors and drew what he saw and also what he imagined.

Soon skunks, bears, and lizards appeared on odds and ends of paper or Christmas cards that Jimmy rescued from the Lippincotts' wastebaskets or found lying around the trading post. Once he painted deer on a piece of brown wrapping paper and a black bear on the torn-off side of a carton. He painted a rabbit on the back of an advertisement from the Liberty Music Shop. Even at the age of eight, Jimmy enjoyed the different qualities of paper and found pleasure in painting colors that came from his desert land, such as chalk-white cottonwood trunks and blue skies.

But Jimmy had his own way of doing things. He did not paint animals in their true colors. He painted green goats, blue rabbits, greenish-gray coyotes, yellow porcupines, mauve does, and blue or salmon horses with fox-like tails. His pictures had rhythm and balance, creative line work, light, but no backgrounds or foregrounds.

The Lippincotts, who had hired Joe Toddy as a handyman, soon fixed up a drawing table for his young artist son at the back of their store. He went there nearly every day after school to paint. Sallie Lippincott, who took a great interest in Jimmy's artwork, made sure the boy always had crayons, watercolors, brushes, and paper to work with. Teachers at the small government day school he attended also encouraged him to sketch. When they took him to see artwork done by older students, he watched them and then set about painting scenes he remembered from everyday life, Navajo ceremonies, and wildlife. This was the traditional Navajo way of learning, observing and doing, rather than receiving formal instruction.

Visitors to the Wide Ruins trading post noticed Jimmy's paintings, and by the time he was 10, he began selling them to tourists. Soon he was making good money for a youngster—even though the prices were set very low, never more than a dollar and usually much less. The boy shared his earnings with his family and friends and with children who had no families. In 1940, a visitor from Illinois arranged an exhibition of Jimmy's paintings at the State

Museum at Springfield, Illinois. All the paintings that Sallie packed and sent to the exhibit were sold. Jimmy, who did not attend the first exhibition of his work, received a check for $11.00. He practiced writing his name so he could endorse the check.

The boy who endorsed the checks had many names, as was the case with Navajo youngsters. In school, teachers called him by his Anglo name, Jim Toddy. Most of the paintings he signed with a variation of his Navajo nickname, Bea Etin Yazz, which means "Little No Shirt" in Navajo. The boy got that name one summer when he spent time painting pictures with German artists visiting the area. One of them, a man who was a sun addict, went without a shirt so the Navajo nicknamed Jimmy "Little No Shirt." The name really was secondhand since it referred to the man's habit of wearing no shirt. The boy used the nickname faithfully, including most or all of the letters that Sallie wrote down for him. Depending on his mood, he varied the spellings. In the right-hand corner of his paintings, he might spell out Beatien Yazz, Beatian Yazz, Beatin Yazz, B. Yazz, or Bea Etin Yazz, or Beatian Yazzia. The boy's real, or "holy," Navajo name was his own business and was not disclosed. According to Navajo custom, the "holy" or "war" names are part of one's personal power. Navajo consider it impolite to use these names in a person's presence because names that have power are worn out by overuse.

The two artists from Munich, Germany, who spent their summer in Wide Ruins took it upon themselves to give art lessons to the little boy. They insisted that he paint on their paper, use their brushes, easels, and palettes, and lectured him about how to use light. Although Jimmy had a shaded bulb as a light source, "No matter how the light fell, [he] practically sat on top of the paper, his dark head bent close over his drawing, and his hair falling down over his face, so that whatever he was doing was completely shaded by his head and hair." Soon the boy grew bewildered with all the instruction and stopped painting because he could not paint the way he wanted. Besides the German artists telling him what to do, his father tried to tell him what to do as well. He wanted his son to copy the pretty pictures in magazines he found at the Lippincotts. Joe Toddy gave up pushing his son to copy after

Sallie told him: "If he draws pictures someone else has done, he won't grow up to be a good artist—or a good man." Sallie did more than defend Jimmy to his father. She took him on trips to Gallup, New Mexico, the Hopi mesas in northern Arizona, and to a museum in Santa Fe so he could see the best of the art that Navajo had done before him. Following these trips, Jimmy drew or painted his impressions.

By the time he was about 11, the young artist had his second one-man show. The La Jolla (California) Art Center gave him a one-man show in November, 1941, that was reviewed by the *Los Angeles Times.* The next year, Alberta Hannum, a friend of the Lippincotts, wrote an article entitled "Little No Shirt" for *Collier's* Magazine. *Collier's* received so much fan mail that Jimmy became a celebrity. Hannum decided to turn her article into a book. In 1944, Viking Press published her first book, *Spin a Silver Dollar: The Story of a Desert Trading-Post,* illustrated with "Color Reproductions of the Work of the Navaho Boy Artist, LITTLE NO-SHIRT (Beatien Yazz)."

Spin a Silver Dollar made Jimmy Toddy a well-known Indian painter before he was 16. Hannum's book offered insight into the young boy's life and painting style. Years later, in 1958, Hannum wrote another book about Toddy called *Paint the Wind,* once again "Illustrated with Paintings by Beatien Yazz."

In 1944, Jimmy enrolled in the Santa Fe Indian School (after studying to be a blacksmith at Wingate vocational boarding school in New Mexico) and due to his celebrity status, he sold more paintings than any other student exhibiting at the Santa Fe Indian School's annual show. At the Indian School, Jimmy finally "learned a little English and it was a good thing. If you got caught speaking your own language you were in trouble." Besides English, he learned about mixing colors and about proportion. After a year of school, Jimmy quit and left to join his father working at the Atchinson, Topeka and Santa Fe Railroad in Winslow, Arizona.

Railroad work came to an end when Jimmy Toddy was inducted into the marines. Fifteen-year-old Toddy got in by lying about his age. He was trained and eventually became part of the

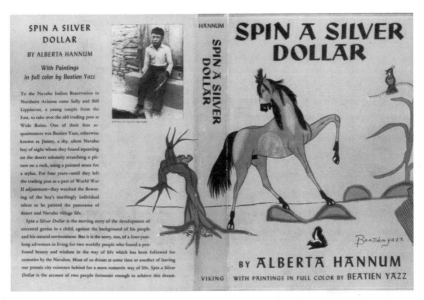

A photograph of the book jacket from Spin a Silver Dollar *shows Jimmy Toddy/Beatien Yazz when he was a young boy.* (Photograph from *Spin a Silver Dollar* by Alberta Hannum. Copyright, 1944, 1945 by Alberta Hannum, jacket illustration. Used by permission of Viking Penguin, a division of Penguin Books USA Inc.)

Navajo Signal Corps. After the war, he was stationed in Tientsin, China, near the Siberian border. Although Toddy didn't paint during the war, he made friends with a young Chinese boy in an art shop who showed him how to block print. When he returned to the United States, his first paintings showed a uniformed marine.

During his tour of duty, Toddy had witnessed three hungry Chinese laborers being shot for stealing food. When Toddy returned to Wide Ruins, he asked the Lippincotts to join him at a ceremony that would cleanse him of the evil he felt watching the violence. Navajo, who feel that witnessing a death will imbalance one's life on earth, have a complex system of curing rituals performed for patients such as Toddy. After the ceremony, which gave him a sense of inward security, he attended others and began painting ceremonial dances. One of these paintings, *Ritual of the Fire Dance*, was eventually lent by its owners to a museum where it was exhibited along with works by Pablo Picasso, a famous Spanish artist, and Jean Renoir, a famous French artist. After he painted Night Chant dancers in 1946, some of the old Navajo men told him he would go blind because he painted a sacred dance. Toddy stopped painting and had a ceremony to prevent the punishment. Although he never went blind, he did have some trouble with his eyes for several months and could not paint full time until his vision cleared.

The Wide Ruins trading post attracted another visitor who had a great impact on Toddy's artistic career. In 1947, James Swann from Chicago, Illinois, came to sketch at Wide Ruins. An admirer of Toddy's delicate watercolors, he arranged for an exhibition of the young man's paintings in Chicago. He invited the teenager to Chicago and showed him copper etching, or printing from a copper plate with a picture scratched deeply into it with a needle. Their relationship resembled the traditional relationship of the teacher who instructs and the apprentice who learns by observing and by trial and error. Swann sent Toddy back to Wide Ruins with plates and a variety of needles so he could make more etchings.

During the summer of 1947, Toddy went to Mills College and studied with Japanese artist Yasuo Kuniyoshi. In 1948, Toddy tried some formal schooling again, one year at the Sherman Institute in Riverside, California, and then two years at the Stewart Indian School in Nevada. While he had been at Mills College, Toddy had started drinking. Years later, with the help of Alcoholics Anonymous and the Peyote Religion, he eventually recovered. Toddy, who had participated in Peyote services before he started drinking, wrote that he "didn't go back to the church until [he] almost died from alcohol. Then [he] quit again . . . The peyote and the doctors helped [him] stop drinking."

Despite the disintegration of his personal life during the 1950s, Toddy began to teach himself more about painting. He watched non-Indian artists work and got ideas from them. He watched people riding horses and looked at how horses ran. The horses he painted became more realistic and showed authentic movement as they trotted, raced, or bucked. After he worked at proportion, the birds he painted had wings in proportion to their bodies.

While in his early twenties, Toddy was selling paintings, but this did not produce enough money to support his first wife, Elizabeth, and their five children. He really started selling his work after he began his own business in the late fifties and sold his paintings through galleries. Museums began collecting his work.

Toddy's artistic style continued to evolve and expand. By the late 1970s, Toddy was experimenting with cubism, a style of art using the shapes from mathematics, lines, planes, angles, circles, and solid geometric forms such as spheres, pyramids, and cubes.

Toddy's paintings now hang in such renowned places as the Philbrook Art Center in Tulsa, Oklahoma, and the Museum of New Mexico in Santa Fe. Jimmy Toddy also gained recognition through numerous exhibitions. He won many prizes for painting at the Gallup Inter-tribal Ceremonial, one of the largest Indian gatherings in the United States, including first awards in 1964 and 1965 and the grand prize for his 1954 painting *Feather Dancers*. In 1970, he took home a first award in the Scottsdale (Arizona) National annual exhibition, an important competition.

In 1983, Toddy wrote an essay titled "Reminiscenses" in which he said that "A lot of people ask me if I have a message to give through my paintings. I just paint what I see." In 1993, Jimmy Toddy lives in the Wide Ruins area of the Navajo Reservation of his boyhood and continues to do just that.

BEN NIGHTHORSE CAMPBELL

◆ ◆ ◆

Northern Cheyenne Jeweler
(1933 – 7♂)

*I call the art world my real life, and I'm not going to give it
up. I want to do public policy, but you must have something
in your life outside politics.*

—Ben Nighthorse Campbell,
New York Times (Nov. 1992)

Ben Nighthorse Campbell, Northern Cheyenne, was born on
April 13, 1933 in Auburn, California. He was the son of Albert
Campbell, a Northern Cheyenne man who hid his Cheyenne
identity, and Mary Vierra, a Portuguese woman born in the Azores
off the coast of Portugal. Raised in Weimar, California, a community of pear, apple, and apricot growers, Ben endured a tough
childhood. Because his father was an alcoholic who worked only
sporadically and his mother—who had tuberculosis—spent 22
years of her life in hospitals, four-and-a-half-year-old Ben and his
older sister Alberta spent a year in a Catholic home for children in
Sacramento, California. In a profile about himself in *People* magazine, Campbell said "My dad, when he was sober, was a good
guy . . . but he'd go on these terrible binges. Sometimes we would
have to turn over drunks in Sacramento on skid row to find out
which one he was." Campbell remembers being so poor that his

mother once split a can of peas between his sister and himself. She drank the juice from the bottom of the can.

Ben did not like high school that much, except for art. "I had always done art as a child, and I began using my hands at a very early age. In fact, any toys I ever had I made myself." Ben was inspired by his father who sometimes made jewelry, a skill he claimed to have learned from Navajo friends. Albert taught his son the basics of shaping, soldering, and piercing metal. By the time he was 12, Ben was making his own jewelry. He said that since he was "too poor . . . to buy materials, [he] would scavenge trash heaps and local dumps."

Besides childhood memories of poverty, Campbell remembers a childhood filled with conflict. "It seemed I was always fighting so I took up judo—legal fighting. At the time, I never dreamed it would open up the world for me . . ." While stationed in Pusan, Korea, during the Korean War, 18-year-old Ben Campbell trained five hours a day, six days a week in judo at a club about 10 miles from his air force base. After leaving Korea, he wanted to continue in judo so he attended San Jose (California) State University, paying for it by working as a fruit picker and truck driver, because it had one of the strongest judo teams in the United States. By the time he graduated in 1958 after studying physical education, fine arts, and business, he was the dominant judo practitioner in the entire nation. After San Jose State, Campbell earned a master's degree at Stanford University in California. At Stanford, his passion for judo monopolized his time. While there, he fought 1,500 matches. This passion took him to Tokyo where he spent four years studying the martial art so he could compete in the 1964 Olympics. "The training I had done in the United States was kid stuff compared to what I went through the next four years." During training he broke his "nose nine times and knocked out two teeth." Even before the Olympics, from 1960 to 1964, Campbell became the Pacific Coast Judo Champion six times, U.S. Open Champion three times, a Gold Medalist in the 1963 Pan American Games, All American in 1964, and finally captain of the U.S. Olympic Judo Team in the Tokyo Games. Despite breaking his knee, he ended up in fourth place and was even able to carry the Olympic Flag during the closing ceremonies. During the four years Campbell lived in

Japan, he fought 50 tournament matches, losing only two. He kept busy learning to speak Japanese, teaching English to support his judo training, and acting in Japanese movies.

After Campbell left Japan in 1964 and returned to the United States, he served for three years on the President's Council for Physical Fitness, coached judo, refereed World Championship matches, and authored a book *Championship Judo: Drill Training*, which is still in print. Ben can thank judo for enriching his life in another way. In 1966, Linda Price took a judo course he offered in Sacramento, California, and ended up marrying him on July 23, 1966. Campbell remained active in judo until 1972. He said, "Having averaged five hours a day for 15 years on the mats, I think I was simply emotionally exhausted."

While he was studying at San Jose State and Stanford, Ben became curious about his Indian identity, but he put off the search because judo occupied all his time. When he was young, he was urged to "never mention that [he] was Indian. It was . . . something to be ashamed of." Campbell, in spite of the warnings he received in childhood to hide his Indian identity, in 1972 began to trace his family roots. "When I finally decided to try and track my roots, I asked my dad who I should go talk to. He told me we were related to the Black Horse family on the Northern Cheyenne Reservation in [Lame Deer] Montana. That's all he could tell me."

Beginning in 1966, Campbell made several trips to the tribe located in the southeastern part of the state to search for his relatives named Black Horse. His search was complicated because the Cheyenne agency housing records had burned in 1958 and the elders of the tribe were unwilling to tell him much. Campbell decided to attend a meeting in 1974 of Northern and Southern Cheyenne chiefs to be held at Bear Butte, a mountain sacred to South Dakota Indians. First he made a gift for the leaders, a ceremonial pipe made from sacred pipestone, adorned with eagle feathers, with a spider web of silver overlaying the bowl. Into this web, he embedded blue turquoise, white mother of pearl, yellow smoky topaz, and red coral to symbolize the four directions.

After the chiefs accepted Campbell's gift (now on display at the Bear Butte State Park Visitors Center in Sturgis, South Dakota), they told him they had traced his background and that his great-grandmother had been killed at Sand Creek, in eastern Colorado, in the grisly massacre in 1864 of a peaceful village of Cheyenne people by Colonel John M. Chivington and the Third Colorado Volunteer Cavalry. Alex Blackhorse, Campbell's grandmother's brother, gave him the name Nighthorse in 1980. Campbell has explained "Black Horse and Nighthorse mean the same thing in Cheyenne but I was called Nighthorse because I had not been brought up on the reservation." Although Campbell never lived in Lame Deer, his father's hometown, his name was added to the Black Horse family and the tribe enrolled him as a member in 1980 and gave him warrior feathers for his accomplishments in judo. Campbell participates in tribal gatherings and wears traditional tribal dress on ceremonial occasions, including a six-foot-long headdress presented to him by the Northern Cheyenne. On August 7, 1985, he was inducted into the Council of Forty-Four Chiefs, an honorary body of both Northern and Southern Cheyenne charged with preserving the tribe's cultural heritage.

After the Olympics, Campbell's interest in making jewelry blossomed. After three years teaching industrial arts in a California high school, he started a jewelry-making class. Over four years, Ben taught more than 100 people, mostly Indians. Many became full-time jewelers. Campbell counseled Indian inmates in Folsom Penitentiary, a high security prison near Sacramento, California. He could not actually help them make jewelry because sharp tools, saws, and files were strictly forbidden, but brought craft materials to show them, including turquoise for jewelry making. One of the necklaces he made while working at Folsom Prison ended up in a jewelry shop in the town of Folsom run by Herb and Peggy Puffer. After telling the owner he had made the piece, she urged him to enter something in the California State Fair. Campbell did just that—and so did 3,600 others—but he "took first prize against all the various forms of jewelry." His winning piece, a necklace, contained handmade beads. "I cut all the beads out of jade, which is a very tough stone to cut." The Puffers, who asked Campbell to bring more of his work to their shop, requested that he sign his pieces. In his role as jeweler, he uses the name Ben Nighthorse.

In 1977, Campbell, his wife Linda, son Colin, and daughter Shanan moved from California to a 120-acre ranch on the Southern Ute Reservation near Ignacio in southwestern Colorado. Campbell equipped his ranch with a jewelry studio so he could work there every day from 5 A.M. (so he can see the sunrise) to noon before going out to work with the horses and cattle. Campbell enjoys "early morning work best, when [his] surroundings are quiet and everything smells clean and fresh."

From the beginning, Campbell had wanted to make a distinctive style of jewelry that honored the artistic expressions of Japanese and Native American cultures. When he lived in Japan, a Japanese sword maker taught him how to laminate together hundreds of thin pieces of metal of different carbon content so they create a pattern right in the metal. The process fascinated Campbell who wanted to adapt the technique to Indian designs. According to tradition, the sword maker did not teach him everything as some techniques were family secrets. Campbell learned enough however. Following the Japanese method, he combined sterling silver, gold, brass, German silver, copper, and red brass into an all-metal form he calls "Painted Mesa," named after the natural colors of the mesas around Four Corners area of the Southwest.

Campbell believes the key to successful jewelry making is the creative design. He sees some designs for his jewelry in his dreams. "I sketch the designs on paper as soon as I wake up." Or he said:

> If I am sitting on an airplane . . . or I am traveling around and can't get to work on a piece for two or three days, then sometimes I will make a little quick sketch and stick it in my pocket to keep it fresh in my mind. But most of the things I make, I just go in cold and start on them.

He also draws on important Indian traditional symbols such as circles, the four colors representing the four seasons, and two more colors representing earth and sky. He signs each piece with the morning star, a Cheyenne symbol, and his name.

In 1979, *Arizona Highways,* an art and travel magazine with readers all over the world, published an issue about the "new look in Indian jewelry." Because 16 of Campbell's pieces were featured,

Ben Nighthorse Campbell making a piece of jewelry at his workbench in 1982.
(Photo by Dudley Smith, 1982. Photograph courtesy of: Photo Archives,
Denver Museum of Natural History, all rights reserved.)

more than any other jeweler, the magazine launched his career.
More magazine stories, news articles, and television specials followed. So have more than 200 design awards for his rings, bracelets, and pendants. Famous celebrities such as comedian Bob Hope
and western writer Louis L'Amour have given his jewelry as gifts.

After he moved to Colorado, Campbell taught classes in jewelry
making at Fort Lewis College in Durango, Colorado. He enjoyed
working with young people, especially with his son, Colin. When
Colin was at about 10 years old, he started working in Ben's shop,
Nighthorse Gallery, a log cabin near his ranch house. Today, Colin,
now in his mid-twenties, and other apprentices complete some of
Ben's work since he now works at jewelry part time.

In 1982 Campbell entered the political arena. He beat a bet-
ter-known candidate by five percent of the vote to win a seat in
the Colorado State House of Representatives located in Denver.

Because he did an outstanding job despite "80 hours a week work, terrible pay, no budget, no staff, and [not being able to] see [his] family," Campbell's colleagues in the legislature voted him one of the 10 best legislators. He kept his sanity in Denver "by setting up a second jewelry workshop and retiring to it in the evenings after completing his daily legislative obligations."

In 1986, he won his first of three terms in Congress representing Colorado's Third District, a mainly ranching district and the eighth largest district in the United States. Through much of his career, Campbell had worn his hair in a ponytail, but before he ran for Congress he cut it. Campbell has since let it grow back, however, because many Indians urged him to keep his hair long. "As the only Indian in Congress, they want me to stand apart, to be different," he said.

Now that he lives in Washington, D.C., Campbell has set up a jewelry workshop. "I have a layout bench and tools there, and I work there when I have free time." Campbell works on jewelry early mornings and evenings, sometimes late into the night. Because of his legislative commitments, he begins pieces in his D.C. workbench and when he goes to Colorado, gives the uncompleted pieces to Colin and other apprentices to finish.

For years, Campbell has sold his jewelry through galleries, museums, specialty boutiques, and trading posts. For 10 years running, he had a booth in the prestigious Indian Market held every August in Santa Fe, New Mexico. Once he became a politician, people came by his booth to grumble about the way he voted on bills. Now, Campbell just does gallery shows.

On November 3, 1992, Campbell was elected senator, the first American Indian to serve in the Senate since Charles Curtis, an Indian of Kaw and Osage heritage, who served in the Senate from 1907 to 1913 and 1915 to 1929. Four days after his election, he appeared at Fortunoff, a jewelry store on Fifth Avenue in New York City, along with other renowned Native artists who were showing and selling their work. He never even considered canceling his Fortunoff engagement. Although fully committed to doing the work of a senator, Campbell calls the art world his real life and he's not going to give it up.

LAWRENCE BECK

◆ ◆ ◆

Inuit Sculptor
(1938 –1994)

I am an Eskimo, but I'm also a 20th-century American. I live in
a modern city where my found materials come from junkyards,
trash cans, and industrial waste facilities, since the ancient
beaches where my ancestors found driftwood and washed-up
debris from shipwrecks are no longer available to me.*
—Larry Beck, from *Mixed Blessings* (1990)

Lawrence Beck was born on May 20, 1938 in Seattle, Washington.
His grandmother and great-grandmother were born in Yupik
villages on Norton Sound, Alaska. His mother, May E. Englested,
born at Unalakleet, Alaska, was a member of the Inuit village
Chanagmiut located on Norton Sound. His father's family came
to North America from Great Britain before the American Revo-
lution. Raised in Seattle, Beck, who was one-quarter Eskimo,
dreamed from boyhood of going to Alaska after his mother's
brother sent him gifts of mukluks (sealskin boots) and smoked
salmon. Beck's family tried to hide the mukluks from him. When
Beck was five, his uncle visited his family in Seattle. After that
happy visit, Beck longed to go to Alaska to visit his uncle, but the

---

* *Eskimo* means "eaters of raw meat" in the Algonquian language. The Algonquian used
the word to insult their northern neighbors. Today, many of the people to whom Eskimo
is applied prefer the name *Inuit*, which means "people" in their own language. *Yupik* is
the term many Inuit living in southwestern Alaska use.

older man discouraged him from doing so. Living a Native lifestyle, in a location that required a boat to get to, without much
contact with Euroamericans, his uncle thought Larry would not
understand his cultural way of life. Shortly after he wrote Larry
that there was "no place" for him there, he died. Beck's dream to
go to Alaska lived on, however.

After attending school in Seattle, Beck studied painting, art
history, and ceramics at the University of Washington, also in
Seattle. After getting his bachelor of arts there in 1964, he stayed
on to study sculpture and get his master's in fine arts the next year.

When he was a student in the 1960s, Beck found himself attracted to the art of the Northwest Coast peoples. These people
developed a distinct artistic tradition expressed in carvings of
animal figures on wooden totem poles, masks, rattles, spoons,
bowls, boxes, and other objects. The masks especially grabbed his
attention, and he spent hours staring at the collections of masks
housed at the Lowie Museum of Anthropology (now called the
Hearst Museum) at the University of California at Berkeley. Some
of the masks on exhibit at the Lowie had been collected by his
Norwegian grandfather in 1890 when he was part of the J. H.
Turner expedition that surveyed the border between Canada and
the United States.

In 1968, when Beck was a visiting art fellow in England, he spent
more time studying Inuit masks at the renowned British Museum
in London. Beck was fascinated with the Inuit masks, which are
believed to be the symbol of spirits that people represent in dancing festivals or that shamans represent in curing ceremonials.
People who wear masks honor the spirits of important animals like
the bear, caribou, seal, and whale. Wearing them, they temporarily
become the spirits the masks represent. Beck noticed the astonish-
ing variation in Inuit masks. Made of spruce or driftwood, he saw
different sizes, paint colors, inlaid ivory, beads, feathers, facial
features, and wooden parts attached to them.

In 1970, Beck, who had studied both Euroamerican and Northwest Coast art traditions, found a way to combine both in sculptural works he called *inukshuks* (the Inuit word for "presence").
About 12 feet high, the inukshuks were made of contemporary

materials such as aluminum and rubber. They were inspired by the Canadian Inuit who left piles of rocks, or landmarks, to aid winter travelers in finding their way across the nearly featureless frozen country of the Canadian Arctic. Anyone lost could take comfort from the "presence" (pile of rocks) left by other Inuit. Inukshuks directly related to the part of Beck that was Inuit, enabling him to draw on his ancient Inuit heritage and express it in a contemporary way. As Beck explained it, "I figured it would be really nice if there were any Eskimos out there on the edge, they would see my pieces and they would say, 'There's an inukshuk there. Isn't that good? Everything is okay.'"

Although Beck was making metal free-standing abstract sculptures of fabricated steel and cast metals, he also wanted to do small-scale pieces. During the early 1970s, a visit to a junkyard in Skagit Valley north of Seattle to look for parts to keep his "dog sled" (Toyota) running changed the direction of his work. Beck told about the moment in the junkyard that inspired him to start making small-scale Yupik mask forms:

> Junkyards are just super places to hang out, if they let you wander around in them. I could spend hours and hours in an auto wrecking yard just looking at abstract forms. The first mask that I cast in aluminum ended up being a traditional oval shape. I saw a similar one on the side of a car. I was far enough away and the sun hit the side mirror on a 1968 or '69 Oldsmobile Cutlass and I just saw this mask there, this Eskimo mask on the side of this car. So I got this idea that I would use the materials that are in my environment as found objects. To me it just made sense . . .

Beck turned the 1969 Cutlass rearview mirror into an Inuit mask by first breaking the mirror, turning it around, so the chromed back of the mirror became the front of the mask, and glued parts of a vegetable strainer around the rim mixing dental mirrors and kitchen tools into the design. For the final touch, he inserted white feathers on lengths of aluminum welding rods. "The soft feathers contrast with the clarity of the chrome and mirrors," Beck pointed out.

The first piece was so successful from Beck's point of view that he did a whole series of animal masks combining automobile parts and other manufactured objects. He combed the Skagit Valley junkyard for every 1969 Cutlass rearview mirror he could get his hands on. "The guy at the wrecking yard thought I was nuts," commented Beck.

Like his ancestors, Beck uses "found" objects from his environment. But unlike traditional Inuit who created masks from "found" pieces of wood that drifted down rivers or animal bones or ivory, Beck hunts for his "found" objects in auto parts stores, trash cans, the Boeing factory with surplus airplane parts in nearby Renton, dental product distributors, and hardware stores selling kitchen utensils. Beck figures it was okay to use dental mirrors, plastic spatulas of all shapes and sizes, multi-colored feather dusters, baby moon hubcaps, rivets (metal pins with heads at one end used for fastening pieces together), razor blades, oil filters, and vegetable strainers in his masks: "If artists back in my ancestors' time had these things available, they would have used them, too." There's another difference, however. Unlike traditional Inuit masks, Beck's masks were not meant to be worn. But Beck does not consider them without purpose: "Everything is functional—visually." He wants his work to have a certain power, or what Inuit call *tunghat,* and he hopes people have a response just looking at his masks.

In 1982, Beck was committed to show new work at the Sacred Circle Gallery in Seattle, Washington. Because Inuit honor walruses, he decided to make a herd of them from auto parts. But it was the work of Inuit ancestors who inspired Beck's contemporary walruses.

> There are real simple walrus masks that are just dynamite. I have pictures of them hanging up here for inspiration, the way some artists look to the work of Frank Stella or Robert Rauschenberg. The man who made those masks is just as great an artist as Stella. But he was a native [Inuit], so nobody remembers his name.

In Beck's world, half-moon chrome hubcaps became walrus faces, coated aluminum rivets became whiskers, and oil spouts substituted for tusks. Beck cut the mouth shape out of the hubcap and outlined it with a strapping used to bind bunches of wires in airplanes. He gave some walruses orange rivet eyes and others small beady grey rivet eyes. The Boeing surplus warehouse, with its bins of rivets in various sizes and shapes, was one of Beck's favorite places to turn up parts for his walrus and other animal masks. He put snow tires behind the hubcaps to support the faces, because, to the sculptor, the tires looked like walrus necks and their texture reminded him of walrus skin. Later, after he got bored with oil spouts, some of Beck's walruses acquired white furniture legs for tusks.

Besides walruses, Beck has made musk ox masks with hubcap faces, spatula eyes, and bicycle-handlebar horns. But sometimes his bear, mosquito, or bird masks, which sport equally here-and-now objects, include a carved wooden piece just like the old masks made by his Inuit ancestors.

Beck may have given his animals modern junkyard parts, but his animal masks carry bicultural-sounding names such as *Punk Walrus Inua* (*Poonk Aiverk Inua*), *Ooger Uk Inua* (*Walrus Spirit*), *Mosquito Spirit* (*Iqtuqyak Inua*), and *Punk Polar Bear* (*Punk Nanook Inua*). In the northern Eskimo dialect, *aiverk* means "walrus," *ooger uk* means "bearded," *iqtuqyak* means "mosquito," and *nanuk* means "white bear." Sometimes, Beck used an Eskimo dictionary for help in naming his masks; at other times, an older Inuit woman helped Beck name them. In 1987 in Phoenix, Arizona, during the Heard Museum's 3rd Biennial Native American Fine Arts Invitational in which Beck was selected to participate, he, too, received an Inuit name. *Aklak*, which means "Powerful Brown Bear," was given to him by David Rubin Piqtoukun, a traditional Canadian Inuit soapstone carver who also attended the Biennial.

Beck's sculptures are popular. Since 1964, his works have been in more than 100 exhibitions. Moreover, he won many awards and honors for his creations. In 1967, years before he made his first mask from "found" objects, he received an Artists of Oregon "Award of Merit" for sculpture. In 1971, he won "First Award" in sculpture in "Art in Public Places," a Washington state-wide competition. His sculpture, a fountain, was placed in Seattle's Occidental Park. In 1973, he received the Pacific Northwest Annual Award

Larry Beck holding Nanook Inua, *or* White Bear mask, *in 1989 while Ki, his husky, keeps him company.* (Photograph courtesy of Alan Berner/Seattle Times)

for Sculpture, and in 1978, received the Anacortes (Washington) Arts and Crafts Festival Award for Sculpture.

Thanks to a number of major commissions sponsored by county and state-level arts commissions in Washington state, visitors to Seattle can see Beck's sculptures installed around that city. His best-known work, *Inukshuk,* a steel sculpture, stands at the new arrivals building at King County (Washington) International Airport. And his works are included in many public and private collections.

Beck's Inuit masks of "Baby Moon hubcaps, pop rivets, snow tires, Teflon spatulas, dental pick mirrors," may have changed Inuit art forever, according to Jim Halliday, the former director of Sacred Circle Gallery in Seattle. While echoing the ancient Inuit masks, Beck "has broadened horizons of what's possible for all Native artists."

Beck died of a heart attack on March 27, 1994. His life was celebrated at a wake in Seattle's Golden Gardens Park, home to one of his sculptures.

JAUNE QUICK-TO-SEE SMITH

◆ ◆ ◆

Salish/Shoshone/Cree Painter
(1940 –94)

In my art I steal from everything; maybe something you've
got on, maybe advertisements or cereal boxes. I put it all in. It
is like a collage, a diary of my life.
> —Jaune Quick-to-See Smith,
> from *Argonaut* (March 22, 1988)

Jaune Quick-to-See Smith was born on January 15, 1940 in St. Ignatius, one of the small towns on the Flathead Reservation of the Confederated Salish and Kootenai Tribes of southwestern Montana. She grew up in a place where meadowlands alternated with mountains from whose tops she could see prairies stretch for miles. Her great-great-grandmother, great-grandmother, grandmother and her father, Albert Smith, were all involved in trading. In a 1992 interview, the artist explained that "My father, a horse trader, was raised by these women, and I was raised by my father." Jaune's middle name, Quick-to-See, was given to her in her twenties by her Shoshone grandmother. "It doesn't mean eyesight; it means being able to grasp things readily." *Jaune,* French for "yellow," came from her French-Cree ancestors.

Albert Smith, whose life revolved around horses and moving around, had a big influence on Jaune's life and artwork. For one thing, the child became sensitive to the beauty of the land, accompanying her father on long horse-trading trips from one reservation to another in the northwestern part of the United States. She became attached to the horses her father trained, developing a close sympathy with animals that later made their way into her paintings. She got used to movement with all the traveling that she did.

An admired rodeo rider and trainer, her father, who could neither read nor write English, struggled to support his family of 11 children. Jaune recalls experiencing hunger and living in 50 childhood homes both on and off Indian reservations, in foster homes when her father was gone, and in one-room cabins. She once said:

> In terms of what you would think of as the average American today, my life was different, yes . . . My father was caught between two worlds. He tried to make a living, on the reservation and off, but without being literate. He couldn't help me with anything.

When the family returned to the Flathead Reservation, she worked side by side with her father splitting shingles, building corrals, and handling horses. She "was raised to go out and round up horses with [her] father, to help [him] fix the fences, and to nail shingles. [She] was expected to do whatever a man could do and nobody ever said to her 'be a little lady.'"

Her father's bunkhouse played a major role in what Jaune saw as beauty. Her father's bridles, ropes, tack, saddles, an old wood stove smelling of smoke remain pleasant memories. The different colors of leather, rope, new or used, and smoke affected her sense of color and taste for textures. She once explained:

> If you'd been raised with corrals and hand-skinned poles being things of beauty to you, with the smell of leather and saddles and Navajo blankets and rugs, with houses made out of weathered wood, with dark colors being a part of your natural environment, then you would probably see the world through different eyes. There were no frills, no lace, no pink dresses, no birthday cakes with pink and white flowers and candles.

Later, her paintings were filled with leather browns, rich siennas, umbers, smoky grays.

It wasn't only the bunkhouse that influenced Jaune. Her father's large collection of Charles Russell prints of western landscapes, traded for over many years, made her aware of art. So did the Navajo saddle blankets, beadwork, and other beautiful things he acquired through trading. When Jaune was a young child, Albert Smith drew animals with great skill. She carried the drawings around in her pocket. Once Jaune's father gave her some roof shingles that he didn't need. She drew a picture for him on the shingle and he kept it hanging by his bed.

By the time Jaune started first grade, painting "consumed" her. She was too poor to buy paints, but the school had easels and little paint cans. She did her first abstract, *Mount Rainier with Children Dancing in the Sky.* Jaune knew from childhood that she wanted to be an artist. With money she earned from the age of 10 working as a farmhand after school, she sent away for the "Famous Artists" correspondence course, her first experience with art education. She used art to entertain and comfort herself and even sold some of her early work. She continued working at a variety of jobs, from horse grooming to advertising, while she went to Puyallup High School.

She got average grades in business courses but was told bluntly that her test scores showed she was not "college material." According to Jaune, that was the usual advice Indian students heard in those days. Jaune was determined to become an artist, however. "That dream had been in the back of my mind since I was six. I didn't know exactly what it meant, but it was when I was happiest. And school was like a magnet, I couldn't stay away," she later recalled.

Jaune's high school diploma meant a lot to her family, but she was set on going to college. But college cost money.

In 1958, when she was 18, she went to Olympic Junior College in Bremerton, Washington. Jaune worked at part-time jobs while she studied to pay for her education. She earned an associate of arts degree from Olympic. There, an art teacher told her that although her drawing was better than that of the male students, she really should not consider art as a career because it was only for men. (Some 30 years later, in 1989, she told an audience of art students about the pain and anguish she felt hearing this message).

Despite the lack of encouragement, Jaune wasn't content with just an associate degree. She persevered for 18 years until she realized her dream of getting a bachelor's degree. In 1976, she graduated magna cum laude with a bachelor of arts in art education from Framington State College in Massachusetts. Four years later, in 1980, after 22 years of moving around the country, attending a string of schools, and working nights and days at a variety of jobs, Smith finally completed a master's degree in painting from the University of New Mexico. She described her struggle, "It took twenty-two years so you see how difficult it was for me. On top of that, I had to raise my three children too!"

At the University of New Mexico, Smith learned about art traditions from around the world and about current developments in contemporary art. She studied the art of Willem De Kooning, Jasper Johns, Joan Miro, Paul Klee, and others. She was attracted to a non-realistic style of painting called abstract expressionism that arose in New York City in the late 1940s. In this style of painting, some of the painters dripped or physically drove their paint onto the canvas. But Smith was equally attracted to petroglyphs, or drawings on rocks, pictographs, old skin robes, ledger art (see chapter on Plains Indian pictographic art), and muslin paintings, all images from her Native American tradition. She saw no reason not to put together the imagery, style, and materials from her Indian heritage and the imagery, styles, and materials of European and Euroamerican modernists that she studied in her university classes. In fact, Smith, who has called herself a bridge between two cultures, feels she is simply acknowledging the reality that she lives in two cultures.

Smith does her painting in a converted stable behind her secluded home on the outskirts of Corrales, New Mexico. When she is there, and not traveling to give lectures, teach, or accept awards, she spends nine hours a day, seven days a week in her studio. Sometimes, her spotted horse, Cheyenne, who pokes his head through the studio window, keeps her company. With her love for Cheyenne and respect for horses that dates back to her childhood,

Smith puts plenty of horses in her works. She claims: "I'm an obsessive worker. More than any artist, I know, I spend more time in my studio."

Smith pours all this time into painting large-scale abstract landscapes that are never static or calm. Filled with the movement of horses, deer, coyotes, porcupines and animal tracks, grass, water holes, fences, tipis, zigzags, horned masks, pottery, arrows, stick figures, geometric elements that appear to be tumbling through space, there is always an indication that activity is going on. To communicate motion and loose spontaneity, she has used accidental drips and splatters of paint, pencil scribbles, and simple line drawings that resemble Plains Indian painted animal skins, shields, and ledger art, ancient petroglyphs painted or cut into stone, and the work of a child.

Smith's colors come from the earth: ochre, gray, burnt umber, sage, and sand. But she also uses exuberant colors. Smith has said about her landscapes: "They are not dead places. The wind is moving, trees are moving, . . . there's movement from past to present to future." Smith also creates richly textured canvases by pasting down pieces of fabric and paper, painting over them with oil paint or beeswax either with thin vertical drips or thicker horizontal strokes. Eventually, one can barely see the pieces of cloth or paper underneath the heavily painted surfaces. Smith also rubs, blurs, erases, blends, and forces layers of paint and pastels into her surfaces. The process makes her feel closer to the ancient way of smearing earth pigments and animal fat together on animal hides. She also identifies with Plains Indian women who traditionally made abstract and geometric patterns in beadwork, quillwork, embroidery, and weaving. (Traditionally, Plains Indian men did narrative and pictographic work.)

Besides creating heavily worked canvases, Smith likes to embed objects in her paintings. She studied and admired the work of German artist Kurt Schwitters who created wondrous art from oddments he picked up here and there—cigarette wrappers, discarded tickets, newspapers, string, wire screen, and whatever caught his fancy. Following his lead (he once said "I am a painter and I nail my pictures together") and also the lead of U.S. modern artist Robert Rauschenberg, another artist who collaged bits of the real world onto his canvases, Smith has made magic with the debris of everyday life. She has embedded ropes, spoons, axes, and nails in her canvases. Recently, she has moved her real-world objects up and out of the picture itself hanging them just above the painting.

From the beginning, Smith has used her art to express her concerns about personal, environmental, cultural, and political issues. The environment ranks high in Smith's list of concerns. In the 1980s, she created her "Chief Seattle" series of paintings to warn people that exploiting the environment would destroy it. In 1854, Chief Seattle of what is now Washington state gave a speech in which he spoke about his people's philosophy of life, how his people were ebbing away before the tide of non-Indians, and how non-Indians disregard the beautiful world that gave them being. In each of these paintings, Smith paid homage to Chief Seattle either with a brass plaque or with C.S. 1854 stenciled into the painting. She placed objects onto the canvases to make certain points. In *Rain*, teaspoons used as raindrops symbolize acid rain. In *Forest*, a real handsaw camouflaged into the picture suggests the eventual destruction of the trees. In *Sunlit*, the eerie light from a single pinkish neon tube placed over the painting suggests pollution. In one work painted earthy green, Smith embedded smashed and rusty aluminum cans and the words "Whatever befalls the earth befalls the inhabitants of the earth." Axes are implanted in other canvases and brushes used to paint rainbows stay fixed on the art surfaces. Proclaiming herself to be crazy about the environment, she's proud that her Confederated Salish and Kootenai Tribe has a stringent wilderness program and a clean air policy. Smith "can still canoe down the Flathead River, where bald eagles nest and dive for fish, and not see aluminum cans or even a McDonald's sign."

Smith is concerned, not only about the destruction of nature, but also about the destruction of Native cultures. In a series of huge paintings called "The Quincentenary Non-Celebration" done in 1992, she targets bad things that white people have done to Native peoples such as giving them small-pox infected blankets and sending children to boarding schools designed to strip them of

Jaune Quick-to-See Smith in front of one of her paintings, 1989. (Photograph courtesy Steinbaum Krauss Gallery, New York City)

their Indian cultures. In *Trade (Gifts for Trading Land with White People)*, which is 170 inches across and 60 inches tall, Smith featured the outline of a nearly life-sized canoe. Above the canvas, she dangled from a line souvenirs that people buy at sports arenas: toy tomahawks, headdresses, Red Man chewing tobacco, a Washington Redskins cap, a Cleveland Indian pennant, an Atlanta Braves license plate, a Florida State Seminoles sticker. Smith has said that if *Trade* could speak, it might say: "Why won't you consider trading the land we handed over to you for these silly trinkets that so honor us? Sound like a bad deal? Well, that's the deal you gave us." The color red dominates the painting, symbolizing "red men," spilled blood, and anger. Peeking through *Trade* and the layers of paint covering other canvases in this series, viewers see countless comics, tobacco and bubble gum wrappers, ads, and fruit carton labels that stereotype Indians covered over with clippings from Smith's tribal newspaper *Char-Koosta*.

Smith's work with its environmental and cultural messages has attracted attention at the highest levels. She was among six artists whose work was chosen for a series of posters celebrating the inauguration of President-elect Bill Clinton. The committee chose her 1989 *Rainbow* in which Smith featured a broad rainbow with its bottom row made of crushed tin cans. Three times Smith has been the subject of Public Broadcasting System documentaries in the United States as well as German and Finnish documentaries. After Smith was the featured "centerfold" in *Scholastic Magazine*, a national magazine for elementary students, hundreds of school children from across the nation wrote to her. She answered every letter. In 1992, she received an honorary doctorate from the Minneapolis College of Art and Design and in 1989 she was honorary professor at Washington University in St. Louis, Missouri.

Smith does far more than paint these days. She hits the road three months a year, lecturing, teaching, and working as a guest artist at colleges throughout the United States. Because galleries at one time refused to accept her contemporary paintings, stating that they weren't Indian enough, Smith founded two artist cooperatives, one on her reservation, the other in Albuquerque, New Mexico. She rounded up other artists like herself who were having similar problems showing their work and arranged 13 group exhibitions for one summer season alone. In addition to all these activities, since the late 1970s Smith curates exhibits, a role usually held by museum professionals. After she chooses a theme for an exhibit, she invites artists to submit slides of their work. Then she selects the art for a show and arranges exhibitions in galleries and museums in the United States and Europe. She finds time to judge art competitions, sits on the boards of directors of several arts organizations, and supports the education of young Native artists.

Smith's work appears in numerous private and almost 40 public collections. Since 1978, she has had 35 solo exhibitions, and, between 1976 and 1993, her paintings have appeared in 122 group shows. Now that Smith's paintings have been reproduced in books and on book jackets, in school curricula, in calendars, and on inaugural posters, many people are paying attention to, and perhaps heeding, her environmental and cultural message.

HARRY FONSECA

◆ ◆ ◆

Maidu Painter
(1946 – 87)

I believe my Coyote paintings are the most contemporary
statement I have painted as regards traditional beliefs and
modern reality. I have taken a universal Indian image, Coyote,
and have placed him in a contemporary setting.
　　　　—Harry Fonseca, from Magic Images (1981)

Harry Fonseca was born in 1946 in Bryte, California, across the river from Sacramento, California. His father is of Portuguese descent and his mother, half Hawaiian and half Maidu, a Native people originally living in California's northern Sierras. The youngest of seven children, Harry, who has said he had "a relatively good childhood growing up" near Sacramento was aware that he was Indian but also equally aware that he was Hawaiian and Portuguese.

Harry spent much of his childhood swimming in the Sacramento River, exploring fruit orchards and hop fields, and drawing. He vividly remembers painting a purple cow on newsprint paper in kindergarten: "If there was a time when I decided I was going to be an artist that would be it." By the time he was 12, he was even more fixed on drawing. It helped him pass the time.

After graduating from Christian Brothers High School, Harry attended California State University at Sacramento where he briefly flirted with the idea of becoming a dentist. The first chemistry class squashed that idea. He then enrolled in a junior college where he discovered the art department: "I didn't realize that there was a whole world of art out there. I was interested in art all the time, but what a delight it was to find out that there were people who supported it." He took classes in color and design, drawing, and painting for two years and then quit to enlist in the navy. After four years in the service, with GI Bill monies, he tried college again at California State University in Sacramento.

When he was 21 or so, Harry started paying attention to his Indian identity. When he found out there was plenty of information available about his mother's people, he studied the scholarly books about the Maidu. Academic books did not hold his interest, however. What he really preferred were the colorful stories and personal involvement with his relatives who he has thought of as "living encyclopedias." He was especially attracted to the old stories that his uncles and cousins told. One uncle in particular, the Maidu elder Henry Azbill, also of Native and Hawaiian descent, greatly influenced Harry's life. Henry Azbill knew both his people's ancient traditions and lived in the here-and-now world at the same time. He devoted himself to preserving Maidu culture, which had endured tremendous turmoil after the tribe was decimated following the flood of gold seekers and settlers onto their lands in the 1800s.

Fonseca reports: "We were conscious that we were Indian, but I was 21 or so when my uncle, Henry Azbill, took me to the dances up on Grindstone (Elk Creek). I really started paying attention to my heritage and it was beautiful." When Fonseca did an assignment in 1973 for an American Indian art class at California State University, he tape recorded his uncle telling the Maidu creation story. Fonseca soon realized that it was much more than a creation story; his uncle was telling the history of the Maidu people. Fonseca has described that telling and other lessons he received from Azbill as

> Something that is positive. Something that is very nurturing. Something that is very solid. Something that is very continuous. Something that is incredibly, incredibly old and incredibly, incredibly new . . . It is profound.

Schooling never pleased Fonseca nor did pop art or other trends of the art world. He dropped out of Cal State in 1971 to pursue his dream of becoming a painter. Art supplies—brushes, canvas, paint, and turpentine—cost a small fortune and at first, Fonseca took jobs as a janitor and business manager of the Shingle Springs Reservation to finance his dream. In 1976, Fonseca applied for and received a Special Projects Grant from the California Arts Council. The monies supported a three-year project that enabled him to produce a series of paintings that visually recorded Maidu oral history. In February of 1977, Fonseca finished *The Creation Story*, his first major piece, which began as a Cal State class assignment and evolved into the visual history of the Maidu. The paintings, which required Fonseca to do plenty of research involving the intricate details of Maidu tribal history, have been called "traditional" because they show Maidu culture—the ritual dances, the regalia, and basket designs of his people. *A Gift from California* (1980) shows four women holding baskets filled with acorns, an important staple of life for the Maidu. He painted each basket with a different traditional Maidu basket design. *Quail Plume*, his grandmother's design graces one of the containers. (This was also the name he once gave his studio/gallery, which he continues to run as the Fonseca Gallery in Santa Fe, New Mexico.) He painted *A Gift from California* shortly after he arrived in New Mexico, a place where he had lived for some years during the 1980s and to which he returned from California again in 1991.

Before his move to New Mexico in 1980, Fonseca painted other aspects of Maidu culture, including some traditional Coyote images. Many Native American people tell stories about the legendary Coyote, a trickster figure with human characteristics who wreaks havoc among humans with his comical adventures. Among the Maidu people, Coyote was responsible for creating the cosmos, people, and the change of seasons. But he also brought about the first death on earth and made life difficult for every living being. Representing both good and bad, Coyote teaches people lessons about their own behavior through his mishaps.

Fonseca remembers the first time (around 1971 when he was 25 years old), he saw the Coyote figure in a kum, a ceremonial roundhouse (sacred structure).

> I was at a sacred dance on the reservation and all of a sudden everyone started saying "there's Coyote!" I never even heard of him before. I looked toward the entrance to the roundhouse and saw a standing figure dressed in a long feather cape and wearing a Coyote mask over his head. He danced around the fire, made some obscene gestures and finally he jumped on an old woman from behind. He . . . ridiculed all of us. I thought to myself that here was something I could use in my work.

Fonseca did just that. He painted Coyote in traditional regalia.

In 1975, however, Fonseca took the traditional Maidu Coyote out of the tribal world, took off his traditional long feather cape, eliminated his Maidu identity, and put mod clothes on his contemporary, playful Coyote figure. In *Coyote Leaves the Reservation, NY NY*, (1982), instead of regalia, Coyote wears urban street dress: black jacket replete with nine zippers, chains, studs, stars, blue jeans, high-top tennis shoes, topped off with an earring. According to Fonseca, Coyote's black jacket is a "contemporary expression of traditional trappings."

That same year, Fonseca painted *Coyote and Rose Doin' It at Indian Market with a Little Help from Gail, Yazzie, and Jody*, which pokes fun at Indian culture in the Southwest where he was living. Coyote, decked out in baseball cap, and Rose, a female version of Coyote wearing a Navajo-style squash-blossom necklace, sell some of the most sought-after turquoise-and-silver jewelry, pottery, and kachina dolls at the annual Indian market held every August in Santa Fe, New Mexico. (Every year the Indian market draws thousands of people hungry to buy choice Native-made art objects.)

In 1983, Harry's urban Coyote took on the most familiar stereotype of American Indians. In *Coyote in Front of Studio*, he wears a Plains Indian-style feathered headdress, sports a black leather jacket, with plenty of zippers, stars, and studs, carries a large beaded bag, and stands on a box holding three cigars, just like the

Harry Fonseca and one of his coyotes in 1993.   (Photo by Mark Kane)

wooden cigar-store Indian statues still positioned in front of some tobacco shops today.

In 1984, Fonseca took his Coyote characters on a new adventure into the realm of classical ballet. Harry had always enjoyed drawing dancers because of their motion and feelings. And he liked to do research. He went to New York City and sketched the dance classes of Dolores Browne at the renowned Alvin Ailey American Dance Center and viewed numerous videotapes of dance at the

Lincoln Center Dance Library, also in New York City. He kept written notes and made small drawings of everything he saw—the dances, dancers, costumes, and sets. When he attended a Lincoln Center performance of Tchaikovsky's "Swan Lake," he jumped to his feet applauding with everyone else when Prince Siegfried and Odette, the Swan Queen, flew off the stage at the conclusion of the ballet. After studying the 1930 film version of "Swan Lake" at the Bolshoi Theater in Moscow, Fonseca felt

> When it comes to "Swan Lake" the Russians have it down. I saw the second act dealing with the swans. It started with a view of the lake followed by a shot of three plastic swans floating across the water. Then the camera backed up and showed reflections of women dancing. It backed up farther and showed the women. They were really heavy, massive for ballet dancers . . . There on the screen were these wonderful dancers with huge legs, who were kicking them up . . . It was just what I was looking for. They looked just like Rose.

After a year or so of research, Coyote and Rose reinterpreted classical ballet in Fonseca's "Swan Lake" series, which he worked on for five years. Rose, in the role of Swan Queen, wears the legendary white, frothy tutu, her heavy legs attired in pink tights. Coyote plays Siegfried, dressed in his ever-present black-leather zippered jacket, blue jeans, and sneakers.

In all these Coyote paintings, Fonseca has experimented with a variety of artistic media: pen and ink, aquatint, lithograph, serigraph, spray paint, and collage. In *Pas de Deux #2* (1984), a painting from the "Swan Lake" series, he glued a curtain of red velvet cloth onto the canvas behind Coyote and Rose. He pasted paper cut-outs to his surfaces in the tradition of Henri Matisse, a famous French artist. He even added glitter to the canvas to make his figures sparkle. In a 1992 interview, Fonseca described how and why he painted the Coyotes the way he did: "My work is pretty much flat, pretty much direct. It doesn't have a lot of technique to it because I've not learned these techniques . . . The *Coyotes* had a directness about them because they were so flat. You always get that direct impact because of that flatness."

In the late 1980s, Fonseca stopped doing Coyote paintings. Around 1988, he began an extensive series of paintings called "Stone Poems" that explore Native American rock images in the West and Southwest. And in 1992, he did a series of mixed-media pieces that are "a direct reference to the physical, emotional, and spiritual genocide of Native people in California." Although Fonseca stopped painting Coyotes for a while, he has begun to paint them again and "they still hold the energy."

Fonseca's Coyotes and other traditional figures associated with Maidu oral history have been exhibited widely throughout the United States, Germany, Mexico, and Japan. In 1978, one of his Coyote pieces took "Best of Show" at the Wheelwright Museum in Santa Fe, New Mexico. In 1986, the Los Angeles (California) County Natural History Museum organized an exhibit "Coyote: A Myth in the Making," a 10-year retrospective of Fonseca's paintings. The exhibit, with some 50 works documenting the evolution of Coyote from the ceremonial Maidu Cayote to the city-Coyote, eventually traveled to the Washington, D.C.–based Smithsonian Institution's Museum of Natural History. It was reported that many people laughed out loud as they walked through the show. This pleased Fonseca, who knows that laughter sets the stage for accepting and learning new things and feels laughing at ourselves is a must. Fonseca's work is regularly exhibited at Fonseca Gallery in Santa Fe, New Mexico, which he opened in March 1993 and in galleries in Chicago, Illinois, San Francisco and Santa Barbara, California, New York City, and Heidelberg, Germany.

RHONDA HOLY BEAR

◆ ◆ ◆

Lakota Doll Artist
(1959 – 9̶3̶)

I feel it is important for others as well as myself, to learn about our cultural past, and the dolls are the by-product of a learning process interpreted in miniature. In turn I hope that my work would stir interest in the minds of others to learn about Indian culture.

—Rhonda Holy Bear,
from *Exhibition Brochure* (1985)

Rhonda Holy Bear was born December 15, 1959, on the Cheyenne Sioux Reservation located in South Dakota. As a child who always felt a creative energy inside herself, she needed outlets. Too poor to buy toys like the other girls, she used whatever was around her to make her own playthings. She walked along the Missouri River picking up pieces of broken glass or whatever else the water washed ashore. With old washed-up pieces of china she found from the river, she made sculptures out of mud. "I've always seen beauty in simple things like a broken piece of china." She found an outlet for her creativity by making dolls. She hiked five miles to the dump to collect bits of cloth and odds and ends that she turned into doll bodies. When she was not making dolls, she was making their clothes. "Everyone had dolls, but I couldn't buy them, so I made them instead." While she was making a doll one day, her grandmother told her a story that further inspired Rhonda's love of dolls. Her grandmother, orphaned as a child, had a doll her grandmother had made for her. She sold her beloved doll, sadly, to a white tourist whose child insisted on having it.

Besides making dolls, Rhonda made quilts. She always enjoyed sewing. She looked at her mother's stitches that were so even, and her own childlike stitches that were so big, and made a vow. Someday she, too, would have the skills to make stitches so little that no one would see them. Years later, she kept that promise.

Rhonda loved beading as much as sewing. When she was 10 years old, she spent time at "Project Light House," which was run by an elderly Sioux woman, Ella Bears Heart, who taught beading. By the time she went to Little Big Horn High School, an alternative high school in Chicago, Illinois, she had been beading for years. She took even more beading classes at Little Big Horn. When she was 18, while flipping through a book she came across a photo of a 19th-century doll with elongated lines and beautiful beadwork and decided to make one like it for her little sister. The project turned out well and because she received "a lot of compliments and words of encouragement," Rhonda decided to continue making dolls. The next step was to look at actual 19th-century dolls, clothing, and other cultural materials of Plains Indians at the Field Museum in Chicago. This museum houses a renowned collection of Native American cultural objects, especially from the Plains areas where Rhonda was born.

On Thursdays, a free-entrance day at the Field Museum, Rhonda Holy Bear spent hours peering into glass cases and sketching the Plains Indian clothing and dolls that were beyond her reach. She next worked her way up to the library where she talked to people about her research. From there, she made her way to the photography department where she saw scores of historic black-and-white photographs of Lakota life from the 19th century. Finally, museum officials permitted Holy Bear to go into the vault. Opening drawer after drawer, she examined both women's and men's clothing, beadwork, featherwork, and horse trappings. She could hold old dolls, feel the weight of beaded clothes, and behold the fine stitching. The names of the artists who created the beaded clothing will never be known, but they left art that made Holy Bear feel proud of her Lakota heritage. Like teachers, they inspired her to create in miniature fully dressed dolls, expressing the incredible energy and spirituality Holy Bear felt in them. In addition to studying close-up the actual clothing and dolls of the 19th century, Holy Bear studied Sioux ledger drawings from the late 1800s (see Plains Indian Pictographic Art and the Kiowa Five). She noticed that besides stylizing the clothing on the figures, the artists drew elongated lines. When Holy Bear started making her dolls, she made them look like three-dimensional ledger drawings. After studying old black-and-white photographs, she made dolls in black and white that looked just like the old historic images.

Doing this enormous amount of research was a must for Holy Bear who wanted a foundation for her creativity and who wanted to capture the essense of a time in history that inspired her. Her passion to get emotionally involved with her work took her to private collections. Collectors let Holy Bear hold dolls close to her heart so she could feel their energy.

After Holy Bear had seen these 19th-century garments worn by women and men of the Plains and Prairie tribes and after researching horses, saddlebags, breast ornaments, and other gear, she skillfully translated the energy of the beadwork, ribbonwork, and other details into miniature form on her dolls and horses. It took her a while to find beads whose size and colors were true to the older garments. She eventually found microbeads, extremely small Venetian beads that met her standards of accuracy.

When making a doll, Holy Bear first makes the body. Some doll bodies have been made entirely from cloth; others are a combination of cloth and wood; some are entirely wood or are constructed with a wire skeletal system. She paints faces with acrylic paint that captures skin color on faces and strengthens the piece. Doll sizes have ranged from four inches to 30 inches tall. After they are painted, Holy Bear works out scale drawings for the clothes. She adds buckskin, cloth, hair, shells, quills, feathers, and bone to the finished garments in designs she has seen on life-sized museum figures or in old photographs. Whatever it takes to make her dolls elegant and historically accurate, Holy Bear does it.

There are some details on Holy Bear's dolls that viewers never see. If the figure she is making wore traditional undergarments, Rhonda adds exact replicas of them underneath the outer clothes. Sometimes she makes painted dresses, one underneath the other,

Rhonda Holy Bear (courtesy of artist)

just the way women used to wear layers of them. The bodies, arms, legs, and feet of her dolls also have tattoos on them just like traditional Plains Indian people even though Holy Bear permanently covers the markings with clothing. The hidden details are just one of the many reasons each doll takes weeks, months, even years to complete. Most of all, Holy Bear prizes her technical skills—the stitching on tiny ribbons barely shows. And a lot of the time people cannot even see it.

Besides her skills at making a single elegant figure, group pieces such as four grass dancers, or horse dolls, Holy Bear is well-known for making "war honor dresses," miniature replicas of dresses that Sioux women made in the late 19th century. The women would cut up the liners of tipis containing the pictorial designs painted by the men to record their exploits in battle, and then make dresses from them. In the 1890s, Sioux women wore the dresses to honor their husbands and sons. War honor dresses are an expression of a woman and man coming together. After Holy Bear hand painted miniature war honor dresses, she took them one step further. Instead of paint, she beaded an entire honor dress, pictorial designs and all. With her microbeads, every detail was possible.

Holy Bear has honored another historic event in Lakota history. In 1889, the Ghost Dance religion, founded by the Paiute prophet Wovoka, spread from the prophet's reservation in Nevada to the Lakota in South Dakota. During an eclipse of the sun, Wovoka had had a visionary religious experience. Taken to the spirit world, he was given sacred teachings that he brought back to Indian peoples. He told them the earth would be renewed, that Indian dead would return to life, and the misery and death engulfing Indians would end if they followed the revelations he had received. By 1890, considerable numbers of Lakota people were ghost dancing. Some dancers experienced trances during which they visited departed friends and relatives and gained sacred knowledge. Holy Bear has made many Ghost Dance dolls. Dressed in muslin garments painted with the religious motifs traditionally employed by the followers of the religious movement, the dolls look inward into another world, searching for strength.

In 1987, Holy Bear returned to her South Dakota reservation. She recalled: "I saw the land where I came from, I walked on the land of the artists of the past. I realized that I carried their blood—they were a part of me." On her trip back, she showed her family a portfolio of her dolls and discovered her people were proud of her

*Doll wearing war honor dress by Rhonda Holy Bear shows the elongated figure
and considerable detail that she prizes.* (Courtesy of artist)

as an artist and as a Lakota woman. She, in turn, gained respect
for her people, and for herself as well. On that trip, she reconnected
with her grandmother and learned that her great-grandmother, a
great beader, beaded to the day she died.

Rhonda Holy Bear's dolls, which have brought her economic freedom and respect, have also brought her recognition and awards from the arts community. In 1985, the Southwestern Association on Indian Affairs (SWAIA) located in Santa Fe, New Mexico, chose her to receive a fellowship, the first doll artist to receive such an award from SWAIA. Her meticulous attention to scale and detail particularly impressed the fellowship panel. The cash grant enabled her to research the dress of Sioux women and purchase rare and authentic materials, such as white duck wings, porcupine quills, and feathers to make dolls.

Father Peter John Powell, an Episcopal priest and historian of the Cheyenne people, adopted by Northern and Southern Cheyenne families as well as by Lakota and Crow people, has asked Holy Bear to restore old dolls in the collection of the Foundation for the Preservation of American Indian Art. With the technical skills she has acquired from years of beading and stitching, she also has restored old buffalo robes.

Holy Bear believes that when she completes each new doll she adds a member to her family, one with a unique presence and energy of its own. Parting with one is difficult for her. But nevertheless, Holy Bear's dolls are making their way into private and public collections. They are now housed at the Wheelwright Museum in Santa Fe, New Mexico, the Sioux Indian Museum in Rapid City, South Dakota, the Foundation for the Preservation of American Indian Art in Chicago, Illinois, and the Kendall Museum in Evanston, Illinois. The foundation has two dolls and the Kendall Museum one doll made by Rhonda's 15-year-old sister, Charlene Holy Bear, already an accomplished doll artist.

In a statement about her art, Holy Bear has made it clear that her main objective is not just to imitate in miniature old pieces of beadwork and clothing. She considers her work not mere imitation for the sake of imitation, but rather "The study of the masters, the art and culture of my ancestors." Her dolls are also an outlet to express what she has learned about her own self, her spirituality, as well as about her Lakota people, all the Plains tribes, all tribes, and finally the whole world.

SELECTED BIBLIOGRAPHY

◆ ◆ ◆

General Sources

Archuleta, Margaret and Strickland, Rennard. *Shared Visions: Native American Painters and Sculptors of the Twentieth Century.* Phoenix, Ariz.: Heard Museum, 1991. An easy-to-find book filled with photographs. However, the essays by the exhibition organizers and others may be too academic for young readers.

Lippard, Lucy R. *Mixed Blessings: New Art in a Multicultural America.* New York: Pantheon Books, 1990. An easy-to-locate book filled with dozens of color photos of fabulous works by artists from many cultures including Native artists Beck, Fonseca, Quick-to-See Smith, and others. Text may be difficult for young readers.

"Native American Art at Philbrook," August 17–September 21, 1980. Tulsa, Okla.: Philbrook Art Center, 1980. This exhibition catalogue, which may be hard to find, has dozens of small black-and-white photographs. Essays are technical and of limited interest.

"One Hundred Years of Native American Painting," March 5–April 16, 1978. Oklahoma City: Oklahoma Museum of Art, 1978. This exhibition catalogue has good photos of paintings, with some in full color. Readable introductory essays provide academic discussions of the history of Native painting until the 1970s. One section discusses "The Art of Ledger Drawings."

Wade, Edwin L. *The Arts of the North American Indian: Native Traditions in Evolution.* New York: Hudson Hills Press, 1986. This book, available in public libraries, contains sophisticated essays analyzing Native art, but many good black-and-white photos (some in color) of artists and their works make it useful to thumb through.

Wade, Edwin L. and Strickland, Rennard. *Magic Images: Contemporary Native American Art.* Tulsa, Okla.: Philbrook Art Center and Norman: University of Oklahoma Press, 1981. This book, which is not readily available, has good photos, with a few in color, of paintings, sculpture, and mixed-media construction. Essays may be too academic for readers.

Dat So La Lee

Cohn, C. Amy. "Arts and Crafts of Nevada Indians." *Nevada State Historical Society, Biannual Report 1* (1908): 75–79. This is an old article that is very difficult to find and not worth the effort.

Cohodas, Marvin. "Dat So La Lee's Basketry Designs." *American Indian Art*, vol. 1, no. 4 (1975): 22–31. This article, in a journal carried by many public libraries, is too technical for most readers. It does contain, however, wonderful photographs of 18 baskets and two photos of Dat So La Lee.

Hickson, Jane Green. *Dat So La Lee: Queen of the Washo Basket Makers.* Nevada State Museum, Popular Series no. 3. Carson City: Nevada State Museum, 1967. A readable biography of Dat So La Lee may be difficult to find.

Stern, Norton B. "Abram Cohn of Carson City, Nevada, Patron of Dat-So-La-Lee." *Western States Jewish Historical Quarterly*, vol. 15, no. 4 (1983): 291–297. The article focuses on Abram Cohn's patronage role in a readable essay. The journal is available in research libraries.

Wade, Edwin L. "Louisa Keyser [Dat So La Lee]." In *The Arts of the North American Indian: Native Traditions in Evolution*. New York: Hudson Hill Press, 1986; 203–210. In a readable style, Wade tells the story of Dat So La Lee's life, minus the technical details of her basketry, and the large part the Cohns played in it. Photographs picture Dat So La Lee, Abe Cohn, and several baskets. The book carrying this article should be easy to locate in libraries.

Nampeyo

Bunzel, Ruth. *The Pueblo Potter.* New York: Dover Publications, Inc., 1972. See same book in Maria Martinez bibliography.

Collins, John E. *Nampeyo, Hopi Potter: Her Artistry and Her Legacy.* Flagstaff, Ariz.: Northland Press, 1974. This is a small booklet cited by several subsequent articles but almost inaccessible.

Coulton, Harold S. and Coulton, Mary-Russell F. "An Appreciation of the Art of Nampeyo and Her Influence on Hopi Pottery." *Plateau*, vol. 15, no. 3 (1943): 43–45. Harold Coulton was the director of the Museum of Northern Arizona, and this is his tribute to Nampeyo written after her death.

Kramer, Barbara. "Nampeyo, Hopi House, and the Chicago Land Show." *American Indian Art Magazine*, vol. 14 (Summer 1988): 47–53. Interesting from a research standpoint. This article provides convincing evidence that an 1898 exhibition in Chicago that Nampeyo is frequently claimed to have attended never occurred. This exhibit is first mentioned in the 1943 *Plateau* articles, and the information is regularly repeated thereafter. This article explains how such an error could have arisen.

McCoy, Ronald. "Nampeyo, Giving the Indian Artist a Name." In *Indian Lives: Essays on Nineteenth and Twentieth Century North American Leaders*, edited by L. G. Moses and Raymond Wilson. Albuquerque: University of New Mexico Press, 1985; 43–59. This is probably the best available article on Nampeyo. It puts her in an historical context and has many quotes from archaeologists and other Anglos who met and admired her. Interesting and available in libraries, this article is academic and has no pictures to speak of.

Nequatewa, Edmund. "Nampeyo, Famous Hopi Potter." *Plateau*, vol. 15, no. 3 (January 1943): 40–42. Nequatewa, a Hopi assistant at the Museum of Northern Arizona, made a trip to Hano soon after Nampeyo died for the express purpose of gathering information on her for the museum's records. This article is of interest mainly because it was used for almost all subsequent articles.

Plains Indian Pictographic Art and the Kiowa Five

Berlo, Janey Catherine. "Wo-Haw, a Kiowa Artist at Fort Marion, Florida." *Phoebus: A Journal of Art History*, 4 (1985): 43–53. An art history journal published by Arizona State University contains an academic but readable essay about Wohaw's drawings.

Ewers, John C. "Plains Indian Paintings: The History and Development of an American Art Form." *The American West*, vol. 5, no. 2 (March 1968): 4–14, 74–76. A journal that may be difficult to locate has a good, well illustrated piece about Plains Indian painting in the 19th century. Ewers covered everything from ancient picture writing on rocks to painting on hides, ledger art, the "Kiowa five," and Oscar Howe. Unfortunately, Ewers's use of terms such as *primitive* detracts from the scholarship.

Peterson, Karen Daniels. *Plains Indian Art from Fort Marion.* Norman: University of Oklahoma Press, 1971. An important study about the drawings produced by the prisoners at Fort Marion has good reproductions and text. This book may be found in public libraries.

Silberman, Arthur. "The Art of Fort Marion." *Native Peoples,* vol. 6, no. 4 (Summer 1993): 32–39. A good source of information, this article has excellent color reproductions and text that readers can easily understand. This journal can be found in many public libraries.

Wade, Edwin L. "The Artistic Legacy of Fort Marion: Beyond the Prison Gate." *Southwest Art,* July 1993, 85–91. The article in this easy-to-locate magazine has good color reproductions and text that young readers will understand.

Maria Martinez

Bunzel, Ruth. *The Pueblo Potter.* New York: Dover Publications, Inc., 1972. Originally published in 1929, Ruth Bunzel's book is a classic. Ruth Bunzel was an anthropologist who gathered her information firsthand. This is a textbook on Pueblo pottery, highly technical and academic and of limited interest.

Marriott, Alice. *Maria: The Potter of San Ildefonso.* Norman: University of Oklahoma Press, 1948. A biography that reads like a novel, written by someone who clearly loves and admires her subject, this book tells the story of Maria's life from her childhood until the death of her husband, Julian. Based primarily on interviews with Maria herself, the book tells Maria's story from her point of view—that of a traditional Pueblo woman in a time of almost cataclysmic change. Wonderful reading for all levels, this book is unfortunately hard to obtain.

Peterson, Susan. *The Living Tradition of Maria Martinez.* Tokyo: Kodansha International, Ltd., 1989. A wonderful book with wonderful photographs, many in color and many going back to the early part of the century, of Maria, her family, her pueblo, and her pots. Written when Maria was an old woman by a potter with a long association with Maria and her family, this is a well-written book about the art, the artists, and the culture. Readily available and worth looking at—even if only for the pictures.

Spivey, Richard L. *Maria.* Flagstaff, Ariz., Northland Press, 1979. Another wonderful book with great pictures, also written by someone with a long association with Maria and her family. Especially valuable because much of the information is told in lengthy quotes from Maria, and they reveal so much more about her than just what they say.

Allan Houser

Eauclaire, Sally. "Allan Houser." *Southwest Art,* August 1991, 66–73, 154. A readable article about Houser's life and art is accompanied by beautiful full-color photographs of his sculptures. This magazine is in public libraries.

Gibson, Daniel. "Allan Houser, Sculptor." *Santa Fean,* June 1988, 16–20. This interesting article tells about Houser's life and includes photographs. May be difficult to locate.

"Houser and Haozous: A Sculptural Retrospective," September 10, 1983–May 1, 1984. Phoenix, Ariz.: Heard Museum, 1983. The first half of this wonderful catalogue includes a biography of Houser and 17 beautiful photographs of his works. The second half tells about Robert Haozous, Houser's son, and shows 16 of his works. Unfortunately, this catalogue may be difficult to find.

Katz, Jane B. "Allan Houser, Apache Sculptor." In *This Song Remembers: Self-Portraits of Native Americans in the Arts.* Boston: Houghton Mifflin Co., 1980. This article, although somewhat dated, is valuable for the insights Houser provides in his own words. Photographs of five of his works are included in the chapter.

Monthan, Guy and Doris. "Allan Houser." In *Art and Indian Individualists: The Art of Seventeen Contemporary Southwestern Artists and Craftsmen.* Flagstaff, Ariz.: Northland Press, 1975, 76–85. A brief biography of Houser's life until 1975 is worthwhile because five beautiful, full-color photographs of his works are included. This book can be found in some public libraries.

Nelson, Mary Carroll. "Allan Houser: Grand Master Apache Sculptor." *American Artist,* November 1980, 80–85, 104–105. This biographical essay of Houser tells about his work habits and shows seven of his works. Interesting details; may be worth locating in some public libraries.

Perlman, Barbara H. *Allan Houser (Ha-o-zous).* Boston: David R. Godine Publishers, 1987. The best source for information about Houser's life, motivations, and studio work habits. There are plenty of photographs showing Houser's paintings and sculptures. Readers should try to find this beautiful book.

Villani, John and Morris, Wayne. "An Interview with Allan Houser." *Southwest Profile,* August/September/October 1993, 14–17. In this interview, Houser shares feelings about working at 79 years old, where he gets ideas, and other details about his life. Photographs show two recent abstract sculptures.

Oscar Howe

Day, John A. and Quintal, Margaret. "Oscar Howe: 1915–1983, Father of the New Native American Art." *Southwest Art,* June 1984, 52–60. This article in *Southwest Art,* found in public libraries, provides a readable biography of Howe and nine full-color photographs of his paintings. Worth reading.

Dockstader, Frederick J. "The Liberation of Indian Art." *Gilcrease Magazine,* vol. 4, no. 4 (1982): 18–25. Dockstader briefly summarizes Howe's life. Seven of Howe's paintings accompany this well-written piece. May be difficult to locate this journal.

―――. "The Revolt of Trader Boy: Oscar Howe and Indian Art." *American Indian Art Magazine,* vol. 8, no. 3 (Summer 1983): 42–51. Dockstader once again summarizes Howe's life, art style, and his challenge of rigid rules that dictated how Indians should paint. This readable article in a journal found in some public libraries also has 10 full-color photographs of Howe's paintings.

Howe, Oscar. "Theories and Beliefs—Dakota." *South Dakota Review,* vol. 7, no. 2 (Summer 1969): 69–79. A technical essay by Howe in an academic journal may not be worth the effort to get through inter-library loan.

Milton, John R. *Oscar Howe*. Minneapolis, Minn.: Dillon Press, 1976. This out-of-print book is an excellent source of information about Howe's life until 1972. Seven photographs show Howe and family members. Worth getting through inter- library loan.

———. "Sioux Artist: Oscar Howe:" In *South Dakota Leaders*, edited by Herbert T. Hoover and Larry J. Zimmerman. Vermillion: University of South Dakota Press, 1989; 409–418. A biography of Howe that deals with the difficulties the artist experienced his whole life, until his death in 1983. Two photographs of Howe accompany this readable chapter in a book that may be acquired through inter-library loan.

Helen Cordero

Babcock, Barbara A. "Clay Changes: Helen Cordero and the Pueblo Storyteller." *American Indian Art Magazine*, vol. 8, no. 2 (Spring 1983): 30–39. This readable article about Pueblo figurative pottery and Cordero's "little people" has photographs of Cordero, her dolls, and the dolls of other artists. The magazine can be located in public libraries.

Babcock, Barbara A., Monthan, Guy and Doris. *The Pueblo Storyteller: Development of a Figurative Ceramic Tradition*. Tucson: University of Arizona Press, 1986. The most important book about storyteller dolls. The authors trace the history of Pueblo figurative pottery, the "little people" first created by Cordero, and the dolls made by other potters. Loads of photos show the amazing variety of storyteller dolls now being made. This excellent book can be found in public libraries.

Bahti, Mark. *Pueblo Stories and Storytellers*. Tucson, Ariz.: Treasure Chest Publications, Inc., 1988. This readable book begins with Cordero's creation of storyteller dolls and moves from Tiwa, Towa, and Tewa Pueblos to Keresan, Zuni, and Hopi Pueblos, offering stories meant to be read aloud along with full-color photographs of storyteller dolls made in the various pueblos.

Monthan, Guy and Doris. "Helen Cordero." In *Art and Indian Individ-*

ualists: The Art of Seventeen Contemporary Southwestern Artists and Craftsmen. Flagstaff, Ariz.: Northland Press, 1975; 16–25. This essay covers Cordero's life until 1975 in a readable style. The details are interesting, and eight full-color photographs make this a source worth pursuing in some public libraries.

Pablita Velarde

Interview with Artist, October 4, 1993.

Nelson, Mary Carroll. "Pablita Velarde." *American Indian Art Magazine,* vol. 3, no. 2 (Spring 1978): 50–57, 90. This article updates Nelson's book by seven more years and shows six of Velarde's paintings in color. Public libraries may have this magazine.

———. *Pablita Velarde: The Story of an Artist.* Minneapolis: Dillon Press, 1971. This interesting biography about Velarde, now out-of-print, is worth getting through inter-library loan. Although it covers her life through 1971, it has details about her childhood, work, marriage, family, and art career as well as pictures of some of her paintings.

Scott, Jay. "Someday It Will All Be a Dream." In *Changing Woman: The Life and Art of Helen Hardin.* Flagstaff, Ariz.: Northland Publishing, 1989; 29–41. A chapter in this book about Velarde's daughter, Helen Hardin, deals with Pablita Velarde's life. Plenty of quotes by Velarde sprinkle the chapter and make it worth the reading. Details about Velarde and her troubled relationship with her daughter show up throughout the rest of the book.

Tanner, Clara Lee. "Pablita Velarde." In *Southwest Indian Painting: A Changing Art.* Tucson: University of Arizona Press, 1973; 168–177. This book that has a brief section about Velarde focuses on the contents of Velarde's paintings. Easy to read, it may be possible to find this book in a public library.

Bill Reid

Duffek, Karen. *Bill Reid.* Vancouver: University of British Columbia Press, 1986. An excellent source for information about Reid's life. Plenty of photographs show the amazing range of Reid's artistic creations. This is worth getting through inter-library loan.

Hoover, Alan L. "Bill Reid and Robert Davidson: Innovations in Contemporary Haida Art." *American Indian Art Magazine,* vol. 18, no. 4 (Autumn 1975): 48–55. This interesting article about Reid's bracelets also contrasts his life history with another renowned Haida artist, Robert Davidson. Several good photos of Reid's work.

Shadbolt, Doris. *Bill Reid.* Seattle: University of Washington Press, 1986. This book contains good details about Reid's life and the way he makes his jewelry and large-scale works. Many good illustrations make this a worthwhile book to get through inter-library loan.

Charles Loloma

Fair, Susan. "Charles Loloma." *American Indian Art,* vol. 1, no.1 (Autumn 1975): 54–57. This brief article discusses the way Loloma makes his jewelry. Good photographs show bracelets and necklaces. Some public libraries carry this magazine.

Lauer, Marjel de. "Charles Loloma." *Arizona Highways,* August 1976, 12. This brief biography of Loloma includes photographs of rings and bracelets. Some public libraries carry this magazine.

London, Phil and London, Anita. "Loloma: The Spirit of the Man in Hopi Jewelry." *Metalsmith,* vol. 11 (Summer 1991): 22–25. This is an interesting article about Loloma's life, along with some remarks by his second wife, Georgia, who clarifies his approach to Hopi jewelry design. The magazine is difficult to locate.

Monthan, Guy and Doris. "Charles Loloma." In *Art and Indian Individualists: The Art of Seventeen Contemporary Southwestern Artists and Craftsmen.* Flagstaff, Ariz.: Northland Press, 1975; 107–110. A dated article about Loloma's life until 1975 does include full-color photographs of Loloma's necklaces, pendants, rings, and bracelets.

New, Lloyd Kiva. "Remembering Charles Loloma." *American Craft,* vol. 51 (October–November 1991): 18–19. An interesting tribute to Loloma because it was written by a close friend of his. The magazine may be difficult to locate.

Stanley R. Hill

Hawley, Carolyn T. "A New School of Iroquois Sculpture." *American Indian Art Magazine*, vol. 15, no. 2 (Spring 1990): 52–55. A readable essay about Hill's life has one photograph of him with his sculpture *The Great Tree*. The magazine should be easy to locate in public libraries.

Hill, Richard. *Skywalkers: A History of Indian Ironworkers*. Brantford, Ontario: Woodland Indian Cultural Educational Centre, 1987. A wonderful history of Indian ironworkers contains readable text, great photographs, and remembrances of seven "skywalkers." The book is worth getting through inter-library loan.

Jemison, G. Peter. "Iron and Antler: The Art of Stan Hill." *Northeast Indian Quarterly*, vol. 7, no. 4 (Winter 1990): 59–61. This article has readable text and three beautiful photographs of Hill's carvings. The journal can be located in some research libraries.

"Stan Hill: Iroquois Art, A Retrospective Exhibition of His Most Important Carvings from the United States and Canada," September 30–October 31, 1984. Schoharie, N.Y.: Museum of the Iroquois Indian, 1985. This exhibition catalogue contains an excellent biographical sketch of Hill plus dozens of photographs of his works. Unfortunately it may be difficult to locate this catalogue.

Eva Wolfe

"Basketry by Eva Wolfe," December 1–31, 1969. Washington, D.C.: Indian Arts and Crafts Board and Cherokee, N.C.: Qualla Arts and Crafts Mutual, Inc., 1969. This four-page exhibition brochure has a brief biography of Wolfe plus pictures of four of her plaited rivercane baskets. Too difficult a source to find.

Dixon, Diane and Domjanovich. "Native North American Cane Basketry." *Shuttle, Spindle, and Dyepot*, vol. 23 (Fall 1992): 40–41. A short article about Cherokee basketry mentions Eva Wolfe. Interesting from a research standpoint because it discusses natural materials and dyes used in basket making.

"Doubleweave Rivercane Basketry by Eva Wolfe," June 18–October 28, 1978. Washington, D.C.: Indian Arts and Crafts Board and

Cherokee, N.C.: Qualla Arts and Crafts Mutual, Inc., 1978. This four-page exhibition brochure with a short biography of Wolfe and pictures of three doubleweave rivercane baskets is another difficult source to locate.

Duggan, Betty J. and Riggs, Brett H. *Studies in Cherokee Basketry*, Frank H. McClung Museum, University of Tennessee, Occasional Paper no. 9. Knoxville: University of Tennessee and Cherokee, N.C.: Qualla Arts and Crafts Mutual, Inc., 1991. This book contains wonderful information about the history of Cherokee baskets, but young readers may find the text too technical. It is worth getting this volume through inter-library loan because it has great photographs of Cherokee baskets, designs, and basket makers.

Hughes, Juanita. "Wind Spirit: An Exhibition of Cherokee Arts and Crafts." Cherokee, N.C.: Museum of the Cherokee Indian and Qualla Arts and Crafts Mutual, Inc., n.d. This exhibition catalogue has brief biographies and photos of Cherokee artists and crafts people. Wolfe and other basket makers are included; may be difficult to locate.

Interview of October 5, 1993, with Betty DuPree, Manager, Qualla Arts and Crafts Mutual, Inc., Cherokee, North Carolina.

Jimmy Toddy (Beatien Yazz)

Hannum, Alberta. *Paint the Wind.* New York: Viking Press, 1958.

———. *Spin a Silver Dollar.* New York: Viking Press, 1944. These two books, both fictionalized biographies, tell the story of Yazz's life from the time he met the Lippincotts, a young couple who took over the Wide Ruins trading post, until he was in his late twenties. Both books are worth reading and each is illustrated with Beatien Yazz paintings. School and public libraries may have one or both of these books.

Tanner, Clara Lee. "Beatien Yazz." In *Southwest Indian Painting: A Changing Art.* Tucson: University of Arizona, 1973; 342–350. This brief section on Yazz gives a short biography of Yazz.

Wagner, Sallie. *Yazz: Navajo Painter.* Flagstaff, Ariz.: Northland Press and School of American Research, 1983. This readable book offers

a biography rich in details about Yazz, his relationship to the
Lippincotts, and his art. It is especially worth getting through
inter-library loan because it contains "Reminiscences," an essay
written by Yazz, and is well illustrated.

Ben Nighthorse Campbell

Hagen, Mary. "A Multi-faceted Man." *Southwest Art*, June 1982, 84–
88. A brief source for information about Campbell in a magazine
housed in many public libraries. There are four illustrations that
show his jewelry.

Hammer, Joshua. "Transformations of the Nighthorse: The Many
Lives of Senator Campbell." *Men's Journal*, vol. 2, no. 1 (March-
April 1993): 100–106, 163. A good article that may be too difficult
for some readers. No photos of jewelry.

Roberts, Liz (Producer). "Ben Nighthorse Campbell." National Native News, October 10, 1989, radio broadcast. This hour-long interview includes Mr. Campbell discussing his jewelry-making
techniques, but is much too difficult to locate.

Staver, Barry. "Rites of Victory." *People Magazine*, November 30, 1992,
50–52. An easy-to-locate popular magazine has easy-to-read text
and a few photos of Mr. Campbell, including one of him at his
jewelry workbench.

Viola, Herman J. *Ben Nighthorse Campbell: An American Warrior*. New
York: Orion Books, 1993.

Lawrence Beck

Hollowell, Jessica. "Artist Depicts Native Heritage in Non-Traditional Materials." *The Anchorage Times*, October 21, 1982. This interesting article discussing Beck's artistic techniques will be
difficult to locate. One photograph shows Beck holding one of his
masks.

"Interview with Lawrence Beck." *Journal of Alaska Native News*. Institute of Alaska Native Arts September–October 1986. This interview
has interesting statements by Beck and a photograph of one of his
masks. Locating the interview will be difficult.

Interview with Artist, September 29, 1993.

Schuette, Rob. "Junkyards Provide Inspiration." *Fourth Estate,* vol. 15, no. 10 (November 16, 1983): 4. This article contains interesting statements by Beck plus a photograph of him standing in front of his steel sculpture, *Inukshuk.* Much too difficult to locate this piece.

Stephenson, Anne. "Place in the Sun." *America West Airlines Magazine,* October 1987, 31–32, This brief article, which includes one photograph of a mask, focuses on the materials Beck uses to make his masks. Not worth the bother locating this piece.

Wasserman, Abby. "Larry Beck." *Native Vision,* vol. 3, no. 3 (July / August 1986): 6–7. This article contains a short biography of Beck and why he took to mask making. A photograph of Beck and two of his masks are included. This may be a difficult source to locate.

Jaune Quick-to-See Smith

"American Indian Artists II: Jaune Quick-to-See Smith." PBS Television, 1982; Half-hour documentary. Worth viewing but may be difficult to locate.

Borum, Jenifer P. "Jaune Quick-to-See Smith." *Artforum International,* January 1993, 87. This brief article discusses Quick-to-See Smith's latest show, a response to the 1992 quincentenary celebration. "Trade (Gifts for Trading Land with White People)" is pictured in this academic reading. May also be difficult to locate.

Clark, William. "Art—Active Voice." *Albuquerque Journal.* August 26, 1990, F1–2. This article deals with Smith's Chief Seattle series and discusses her environmental activism. Three of her paintings are pictured, but the writing is academic and the newspaper may be difficult to locate.

Herzog, Melanie. "Building Bridges Across Canada: Jaune Quick-to-See Smith." *School Arts,* October 1992, 31–34. This article directed at art teachers may be too academic for young readers. There is a good photograph of a painting from the Chief Seattle series as well as a discussion about it.

Hurst, Tricia. "Crossing Bridges: Jaune Quick-to-See Smith, Helen Hardin, Jean Bales." *Southwest Art,* April 1981, 82–91. Part of this article provides a statement by Smith about what it feels like to be a woman, artist, and Indian, as well as a brief biography about her. Interesting to read with a few of her paintings pictured. The magazine is in public libraries.

"Jaune Quick-to-See Smith," January 17–March 14, 1993. Norfolk, Virginia: Chrysler Museum, 1993. A wonderful exhibition brochure owing to the full-color photographs of her recent series of paintings confronting the quincentenary of 1992. The text is technical and the curriculum vitae may be of little interest to young readers. Also, the brochure will be difficult to locate.

Pierik, Dave. "Vitality Found in Native American Art." *Argonaut* (Associated Students of University of Idaho), March 22, 1988.

Harry Fonseca

Abbot, Larry. "Giving Visual Form to Myth: An Interview with Maidu Artist Harry Fonseca." *Akwe:kon Journal*, vol. 10, no. 2 (Summer 1993): 4–15. In this long interview with Fonseca, he discusses his Coyote series and his more recent *Stone Poems and Discovery of Gold and Souls in California* series. Photographs of two coyote paintings, five paintings from his Stone Poems series, two Magic Boxes, and Fonseca photographed in front of his *Discovery* series accompany the interview. Good reading in a journal that may be tough to locate.

Archuleta, Margaret. "Coyote: A Myth in the Making." Washington, D.C.: National History Museum Foundation, 1986. A wonderful exhibition brochure with a biography of Fonseca and full-color reproductions of early work and four Coyote paintings. This may be tough to find.

Interviews with Artist, September 30, 1993 and October 12, 1993.

Jones, Don H. "Harry Fonseca." *Santa Fean*, August 1984, 55–57. This brief biography of Fonseca is easy to read. It may not be worth searching for because it lacks illustrations.

LaPena, Frank. "Coyote: A Myth in the Making. An Interview with Harry Fonseca." *News from Native California*, vol. 1, no. 5 (November–December 1987): 18–19. In this brief interview, Fonseca discusses his Coyote exhibition. One of his Coyote dancers is pictured. This journal may be tough to locate.

————. "Rights and Symbols." *News from Native California*, vol. 6, no. 2 (Spring 1992): 4–5. In this article, LaPena mentions Fonseca's exhibition "A Gift from California—the Maidu Creation Story."

LaPena, Frank R. and Driesbach, Janice T., eds. "The Extension of Tradition: Contemporary Northern California Native American Art in Cultural Perspective." Sacramento, Calif.: Crocker Art Museum, 1985. One page in this exhibition catalogue has a brief biography of Fonseca and shows one coyote painting. Too difficult to locate.

Wilson, Darryl. "Harry Fonseca." *News from Native California,* vol. 7, no. 1 (Winter 1992/1993): reverse of unpaged poster. In this brief biography of Fonseca, Wilson focuses on the important role of Fonseca's uncle, Henry Azbill, in Fonseca's life and art. The artist is pictured in his studio. This journal may be difficult to locate.

Rhonda Holy Bear

"Dolls by Bernice Alderman and Rhonda Holy Bear," March 24 to May 3, 1985. Rapid City, S.D.: Sioux Indian Museum and Crafts Center, 1985. This four-page exhibition brochure shows Holy Bear and two of her dolls. A brief biography is included in this difficult-to-locate item.

Hammond, Harmony and Smith, Jaune Quick-to-See. "Rhonda Holy Bear." In "Women of Sweetgrass, Cedar, and Sage: Contemporary Art by Native American Women." New York: American Indian Community House Gallery, 1985. A short readable statement by Holy Bear is included in this important exhibition catalogue. A difficult source to locate.

Hill, Richard. "Indian Art: Swimming in the Mainstream." *Daybreak,* Spring 1988, 19–20. This article has good information about Holy Bear's art, plus one photograph of a Ghost Dance doll, but it will be difficult to track this journal down.

Holy Bear, Rhonda. "Biographical Information." Phoenix, Ariz.: Heard Museum, 1986. The Phoenix-based Heard Museum provides biographical information about artists to researchers. In 1986, Holy Bear filled out a questionnaire when she took part in a "Crafts Arts Invitational" at the Heard.

Interviews with Artist, October 8, 1993 and October 20, 1993.

Kusel, Denise. "Rhonda Holy Bear." *Dolls: The Collectors' Magazine,* September-October 1986, 40. This brief article has some interesting details about Holy Bear's doll art and one photograph, but the magazine will probably be hard to locate.

Libhart, Nyles. "To Dress with Great Care: Contemporary American Indian and Eskimo Doll Artists of the United States." *American Indian Art Magazine,* vol. 14, no. 2 (Spring 1989): 38–51. There is a brief mention of Holy Bear in this excellent article that surveys Native doll artists. Two of Holy Bear's Ghost Dance dolls photographed in full color grace the cover of the journal. *American Indian Art Magazine* can be found in public libraries.

Mayeux, Lucie. "SWAIA Fellowships for 1985." *Artists of the Sun,* August 14, 1985, 57. This brief article, with a photograph of Holy Bear holding one of her dolls, is of interest mainly because it mentions her 1985 fellowship from the Southwestern Association on Indian Affairs.

"Rhonda Holy Bear." *America West Quarterly Newsletter,* vol. 2 (Fall 1982): 5. This newsletter contains brief mention of Holy Bear who was exhibiting at America West in Chicago in 1982. There is one photograph of Holy Bear with five of her dolls. Much too difficult to locate this item.

INDEX

Boldface type indicates main headings.
Italic numbers indicate illustrations.